Praise for *The Talent Era*

"It is not very often that a book comes along that shakes your assumptions about people management and how it works. Subir Chowdhury's *The Talent Era* is that kind of book: powerful and brilliant. At a time when Talent is the scarcest and most costly resource for most organizations, this book provides insights as to how you can maximize your investment and potential in your people. All managers and leaders should read this book!"

—BOB NELSON
Best-selling author of 1001 Ways to Reward Employees
and Please Don't Just Do What I Tell You! Do What Needs to Be Done

"People are the most important resource of any organization. Recruiting, developing, and keeping talented people is a formula for success. Chowdhury provides the leader with a special insight into the why's and how to's of accomplishing this important task."

—C. WILLIAM POLLARD
Chairman, The ServiceMaster Company

"In times of crisis, managing a meritocracy is critical. A company must have the best talent, and it must rise to the top. Chowdhury's *The Talent Era* tells just how to make that happen."

—JAMES CHAMPY
Chairman of Consulting, Perot Systems
Co-author, Reengineering the Corporation

"Subir Chowdhury has hit the nail on the head with this book that focuses on the value of talent in any organization today. Management has always had to deal with talented people, but heretofore they have been focusing on how to keep such talented individuals from causing too much disruption to the rest of the organization. Today, our focus needs to be more on how to move the rest of the organization to benefit from such constructive disruption, which is necessary in today's fast-changing and competitive environment."

—J. D. POWER III
Chairman and Founder, J. D. Power and Associates

"Subir Chowdhury has done it again! *The Talent Era* confirms Chowdhury is one of the most practical thought leaders in business today. *The Talent Era* is the guidebook for talent management in our new world."

—MARSHALL GOLDSMITH
Co-founder, Financial Times Knowledge Dialogue
Co-editor, The Leader of the Future *and* Coaching for Leadership

"You may not think of yourself as 'talent,' someone deserving of all the attention that those superstars get. After you read Subir Chowdhury's *The Talent Era* you'll change your mind. Every one of us is gifted in some way, and every one of us will find Chowdhury's messages extraordinarily beneficial in developing our careers and living our lives. Organizational leaders must take Chowdhury's lessons to heart. Organizations will soar when all employees are treated the way Chowdhury convincingly argues they should be. This book is profoundly important to moving beyond present challenges and creating organizations that are alive with creativity, energy, and enthusiasm."

—JAMES M. KOUZES
Co-author, The Leadership Challenge, *Chairman emeritus, Tom Peters Company*

"Attracting and retaining talent is the most important issue for business leaders today. Chowdhury's book identifies intelligent responses to these daunting organizational challenges. Those organizations valuing and respecting 'human capital' will have a vast head start in creating cultures that can withstand the turmoil of today's chaotic and unpredictable economy."

—STUART R. LEVINE
Chairman and CEO, Stuart Levine & Associates, LLC
Former CEO, Dale Carnegie and Associates, Inc.

"This is an extraordinarily valuable book. Chowdhury does an amazing job of spelling out how to handle the biggest challenge facing all managers these days: getting, keeping, and maximizing the value of talented people. His simple, easy-to-follow, common-sense but not common-practice ideas are pure gold. This is must reading for any leader in any organization."

—JAMES A. BELASCO
Best-selling author, Teaching the Elephant to Dance *and* Flight of the Buffalo

"Subir Chowdhury's *The Talent Era* is a 'must read' for any human resource professional or line manager who is challenged by the talent issues in the workplace. Chowdhury explains, in a most 'make sense' way, the essential ingredients for recognizing, rewarding, and utilizing talent in today's economy. This book is a critical manual for remaining competitive in the marketplace."

—BEVERLY KAYE
President and founder, Career Systems International
Co-author, Love 'Em or Lose 'Em: Getting Good People to Stay

"*The Talent Era* does what no one has done before — quantify, measure, and place an analytic and financially recognizable process onto the subjective and vague subject of Talent. Subir Chowdhury has done it again — a must-have for any company on the cutting edge of innovation."

—LARRAINE SEGIL
Author, Intelligent Business Alliances *and* Fast Alliances: Power your E-business

THE TALENT ERA

ISBN 0-13-041040-3

9 790130 410404

90000

FINANCIAL TIMES PRENTICE HALL BOOKS

For more information, please go to www.ft-ph.com

Deirdre Breakenridge
Cyberbranding: Brand Building in the Digital Economy

Jonathan Cagan and Craig M. Vogel
Creating Breakthrough Products: Innovation from Product Planning to Program Approval

Subir Chowdhury
The Talent Era: Achieving a High Return on Talent

Sherry Cooper
Ride the Wave: Taking Control in a Turbulent Financial Age

James W. Cortada
21st Century Business: Managing and Working in the New Digital Economy

James W. Cortada
Making the Information Society: Experience, Consequences, and Possibilities

Aswath Damodaran
The Dark Side of Valuation: Valuing Old Tech, New Tech, and New Economy Companies

Sarvanan Devaraj and Rajiv Kohli
The IT Payoff: Measuring the Business Value of Information Technology Investments

Jaime Ellertson, Charles W. Ogilvie, and Andrew Ladd
Frontiers of Financial Services: Turning Customer Interactions Into Profits

Nicholas D. Evans
Business Agility: Strategies for Gaining Competitive Advantage through Mobile Business Solutions

David Gladstone and Laura Gladstone
Venture Capital Handbook: An Entrepreneur's Guide to Raising Venture Capital, Revised and Updated

David R. Henderson
The Joy of Freedom: An Economist's Odyssey

Dale Neef
E-procurement: From Strategy to Implementation

John R. Nofsinger
Investment Madness: How Psychology Affects Your Investing… And What to Do About It

Tom Osenton
Customer Share Marketing: How the World's Great Marketers Unlock Profits from Customer Loyalty

Stephen P. Robbins
The Truth About Managing People … And Nothing but the Truth

Jonathan Wight
Saving Adam Smith: A Tale of Wealth, Transformation, and Virtue

Yoram J. Wind and Vijay Mahajan, with Robert Gunther
Convergence Marketing: Strategies for Reaching the New Hybrid Consumer

THE TALENT ERA

ACHIEVING
A HIGH RETURN
ON TALENT

Subir Chowdhury

FINANCIAL TIMES
Prentice Hall

An Imprint of Pearson Education
London • New York • San Francisco • Toronto • Sydney
Tokyo • Singapore • Hong Kong • Cape Town • Madrid
Paris • Milan • Munich • Amsterdam

Library of Congress Cataloging-in-Publication Data

A CIP catalog record for this book can be obtained from the Library of Congress.

Editorial Production/Composition: *G & S Typesetters, Inc.*
Acquisitions Editor: *Jim Boyd*
Marketing Manager: *Bryan Gambrel*
Manufacturing Manager: *Maura Zaldivar*
Cover Design Director: *Jerry Votta*
Cover Design: *Nina Scuderi*
Art Director: *Gail Cocker-Bogusz*
Interior Design: *Tech Graphics*
Project Coordinator: *Anne R. Garcia*

FINANCIAL TIMES
Prentice Hall

© 2002 by Subir Chowdhury
Published by Prentice Hall PTR
Prentice-Hall, Inc.
Upper Saddle River, NJ 07458

Prentice Hall books are widely used by corporations and government agencies for training, marketing, and resale.

The publisher offers discounts on this book when ordered in bulk quantities.
For more information, contact: Corporate Sales Department, Phone: 800-382-3419;
Fax: 201-236-7141; E-mail (Internet): corpsales@prenhall.com; or write Prentice Hall PTR, Corp. Sales Dept., One Lake Street Upper Saddle River, NJ 07458

Printed in the United States of America

10 9 8 7 6 5 4 3 2 1

ISBN 0-13-041040-3

Pearson Education Ltd.
Pearson Education Australia PTY, Ltd.
Pearson Education Singapore, Pte. Ltd.
Pearson Education North Asia Ltd.
Pearson Education Canada, Ltd.
Pearson Educación de Mexico, S.A. de C.V.
Pearson Education — Japan
Pearson Education Malaysia, Pte. Ltd.

For Anandi,
my own little talent of love,
and
for Malini,
whose convincing arguments helped me to write *The Talent Era*.

Contents

Introduction:
Welcome to the Talent Era

It was late 1969, and the Amazing Mets had just won the World Series. The United States was in a turbulent time. The civil rights movement, the assassinations of Martin Luther King and Robert Kennedy, and the moon landing dominated the headlines. Riots had erupted across the country; music, theater, movies, and TV shows explored uncensored territory; and, yes, the Mets had won. The world had turned upside-down. But of all those events in the late sixties, the one that might seem inconsequential had one of the biggest impacts in the long term. You see, it was the Mets rather than the Cardinals who won the National League championship.

Throughout the 1960s, the Cardinals had been a powerhouse. In 1969, the Cardinals had won three of the previous five years and were expected to win again. They had Bob Gibson, Lou Brock, and several other fine players. But the Cardinals had been ruled with an iron fist, and one outstanding player voiced a complaint that had been brewing for years. Curt Flood was one of the greats: He was a three-time all-star, played a record 226 games without an error, was awarded seven Gold Gloves, and was a lifetime .293 hitter in an era when pitchers dominated. With Flood, the Cards had won three National League pennants and two World Series. It was his eleventh year in the league in 1969. Whereas Flood was making $90,000 at the time, many players were making less than $10,000. Under baseball's reserve clause — which had been in effect in one form or another since the game began — a team owned a player. If a player would not sign an agreement with his team, he had the option of quitting baseball, but he could not play for another team. Players were traded from team to team, sometimes against their wishes. This was the way it was, and, although many had grumbled about it, no one had tried to buck the system. But after losing the pennant in 1969, the Cards, who viewed Flood as a troublemaker despite his obvious skills, decided to trade him to the Phillies. Flood refused to go and on January 16, 1970, filed a lawsuit claiming that the reserve clause violated the antitrust act and should be eliminated. In the end, Flood lost the suit. He sat out the 1970 season and was traded to the Washington Senators in 1971. After thirteen games, he decided the atmosphere was too difficult and retired from the game. But the damage had been done — Flood's suit had broken the dam. In 1975 it was official: Andy Messersmith and Dave McNally won their case against the reserve clause, and *free agency* was born.

In 1976, the average baseball player received eight times what the average person received in compensation. By 1994, baseball salaries had reached fifty times the average salary. Free agency had changed the game, other sports, and everyone's perception of what a worker was worth. No longer were wages a suppressed topic that management dictated. Curt Flood cut his career short based on his conviction that he was in effect a slave to baseball and that he should be free to go out and seek whatever employment he could. He had seen the impact of free agency not only on the game of baseball, but also in every walk of life.

But Flood had opened up the gates. His action opened a new era — an era when people evaluate their own talent and expect to get what they are worth. At first, it was confined to sports. Basketball players quickly figured out that there are only five guys out there generating a lot of revenue, and so they ought to be paid for it. Football followed suit. Soon each top tennis player, each top golfer, each top player in any sport is a very visible Talent (in this book we will capitalize the word *Talent* when referring to a person with talent).

It should be pointed out that in the entertainment business, Talents have always been paid *much* more than others in their craft. It used to be that the studios ruled and had their actors under contract, much as did Major League Baseball. But there was generally the possibility that another studio would pick up the renegade actor. It was Cary Grant who actually bucked the studio system, but the repercussions of his actions were confined to the entertainment industry and did not affect the world at large.

Not Just Sports and Entertainment Anymore

Just as athletes and entertainers had felt the effects of free agency early, in the 1990s talented workers in many other fields began to understand their real worth to their organizations. Management may have known it all along: All workers are free agents. Companies tried for years to foster the feeling that people were there to work for life, and they would be paid whatever management felt like giving them — and they would have to take it. It was as if a self-imposed reserve clause existed. Management tried to build loyalty by dispensing more incentives, but this system began to break down as more people started to see themselves as Talent, as free agents who should receive more if they produced more.

Ironically, corporations often foolishly broke the bond of trust through massive layoffs and an indifferent attitude toward their employees. Even IBM, which typified the "you are here for life" attitude, was among the first in the "lay off people to boost your stock price" movement of the 1980s. This seemingly callous attitude toward employees was headline news, but it happened so regularly that by the 1990s, work for many people had become a place to go simply to make money — it was no longer a home away from home. Loyalty was a zero-sum game. It was not unusual to see people moving every year to a new job, enabled by the Internet and other information technologies. With the growth in the economy, new ventures opened up every day. It was a time to keep your eyes open for new opportunity.

When the big Internet blitz hit, getting into the game early often meant millions of dollars. Getting the best Talent to generate the best ideas and products meant future market domination. Suddenly, all in-demand workers were like free agents. The stories of Steve Ballmers of Microsoft driving up to the front door of Borland with million-dollar signing bonus checks for Borland's key Talents — and then driving away with them — may or may not be true, but many of these people now work for Microsoft. The so-called "Talent war" was on.

Although the "war" may have ended, today we are still in the midst of the *Talent Era*. People are more aware than ever of their value to their company. So, management must now identify its key Talents, attract more Talents, grow Talents, manage and motivate Talents, and keep Talents. Success depends on these Talent management skills.

This book will teach you all you need to know if you are a Talent, if you manage Talent, or if you hope to optimize the Talent in your organization. This era is defined by a basic change in relationship between employees and companies. Most employees today have lost their dedication to their company. In the face of increased layoffs and the fact that employees will change jobs if another "situation" looks better, any company that wants to be successful needs to adapt, to anticipate losing Talent, to foster more Talent, to try to keep the Talent it has, and to make sure this Talent is utilized to the fullest. Those less-talented employees, including many knowledge workers, may still be vital to keep the company going, but they need to be compensated differently.

That is a key tenet of this book — that top Talents should be compensated commensurate with their contributions and that companies must adapt to this framework to succeed. Because Talent can be found at any level, if you are paying everyone what you pay to keep Talent, you will quickly find yourself in an untenable position. Likewise, if you are a talented person, you want to work for a company that will recognize your ability and not tell you that everyone at your level gets treated the same — even if you are doing the work of three people or have just developed the product that will save the company.

In the Talent Era, the "flood gates" are open. Just as most athletes and entertainers would not want to go back to the old days, most talented business employees would not want to go back to lifetime employment contracts. Companies can do a lot more to keep Talent, but after the ideals of self-determination, capitalism, and freedom to choose are embraced by people, companies must adapt to the situation at hand. Tough decisions need to be made. Talent-friendly policies and practices may be the difference between success and failure. The Talent Era clearly won't end anytime soon. And so, every manager needs to understand the implications.

The Effects of Free Agency

Team owners know that people go to games to watch the marquee players. Look at the interest that was generated in baseball by the Mark McGwire–Sammy Sosa home run race and again with Barry Bonds. Even more intense is the attention garnered by Tiger

Woods in golf. Tiger has put excitement back into golf. Throughout the history of sports, there have always been high-impact players, the all-stars. The same is true in entertainment. Big names bring in big bucks. Stars sell movies. Bigtime directors and producers like Steven Spielberg or George Lucas put people into the seats. Big-draw names can mean tens of millions in revenue for a single movie. In some sports and most entertainment, however, if you are not a marquee Talent, you may be a poor, starving artist.

But in baseball, even the worst players make exceptional money — and that is where management made its mistake. The owners' initial reaction to free agency was predictable: They went out and bid up the cost of the good players, and thus their payrolls shot up. The money spent for the best players became a draw in and of itself. The owners with the most money tended to win the most games. But to make up for their monetary losses, the owners increased ticket prices, boosted advertising and promotions in the ballparks, licensed souvenirs with their logos, and negotiated more lucrative TV contracts.

If baseball owners had paid their stars commensurate with their contributions and left it at that, then we might say that these were smart business decisions needed to compete and fill stadium seats. But, baseball owners failed to understand the difference between Talent and knowledge workers, between stars and utility players. People go to the game, read the paper, watch the news, view sports shows, and listen to radio shows to keep up with the players who win games through their ability. They are worth more money. The difference between a star and an average player is substantial. Average players can be easily replaced. Where owners make their mistake — in sports and in business — is when they start paying average players substantially more. The median baseball salary is now over $1 million. Eventually, this "salary creep" spreads to players who could be replaced by any of dozens of minor leaguers who are getting paid substantially less.

Minimum salary levels have skyrocketed since free agency began. The impact has been highly inflationary. Owners could contract most players for much less, but they seem not to understand: Treat your stars differently. Why should a fifth-place team be paying a mediocre pitcher $5 million to lose fifteen games? Obviously, you try to do your best, but the return on your investment needs to be there.

The Impact of Unions

The labor unions in baseball gained great power with the advent of free agency. The threat and the actuation of strikes had a major impact on the agreements between owners and players. Indeed, the union is a major reason for the high minimum salary now afforded to baseball's weakest players. So far, baseball owners have afforded the costs, in part by raising prices and taking smaller profits. They have bowed to union demands. Other sports unions, especially in basketball and football, have had similar success, based largely on the visibility of the Talent.

But unions have had little impact on the highest salaries paid to the stars. In fact, in most sports, unions have somewhat suppressed the money available to stars in favor of utility players. The unions' work is largely based on raising minimums — and getting the stars to go along.

So, we might suppose that unionization might be the best approach for workers in general and perhaps even for Talent. Unions have historically fought for minimum wage levels, treating employees at certain levels equally, and demanding benefits. If a corporation is unionized, it may be hesitant to offer employees new incentives, fearing that they may become permanent and more widespread. Certainly, offering employees at a given level more than other employees at that level is likely to signal to a union that the corporation is in a position to pay more for those employees. A corporation may become reluctant to offer new programs to keep Talents, especially if it is in a competitive market where increases in costs might jeopardize the corporation. By mandating pay scales and quotas, unions may hamper management's ability to treat Talent differently. In fact, unionization generally forces companies not to respond to the needs of Talent, and so the best Talents leave. Over time, this breeds mediocrity and failure. With no one putting pressure on salaries, everyone remains on the low end, and the corporation remains flat and uncompetitive.

In essence, where unions succeeded in baseball, they could fail in a competitive marketplace. The unions took advantage of the Talents' increase in salaries to drive up the salaries of the utility players in baseball. The lesson to the unions here is to allow the Talents to get the increases and hope that those increases will drive the salary levels of all workers. If unions push for the best people to get paid better and argue that their workers should be compensated in line with any other worker, as has happened in sports, they may get the best of both worlds. This seems unlikely to happen, and so unionization may stifle the upward salary movement that is being generated in the Talent Era.

The End Game

Indeed, in 2001, the strong demand for Talent over the past three years resulted in major wage increases. The pressure on salaries for Talent is driving salaries up for everyone. Clearly, corporations are feeling the pressure from the Talent and are reacting as many owners of sports teams have — by paying more for everyone.

If business owners let themselves or unions dictate universal salary structures, then corporations, in defending key Talent, will be forced to boost the salary structures for everyone. This is what happened in professional sports, and it is happening in almost every corporation worldwide. The effect is that much of the workforce is becoming overpaid. In economic downturns, this portends massive layoffs. In turn, a company then does not have the knowledge workers it needs and is hampered by insufficient staffing. Every corporation should want its employees to be compensated properly in relation to their return on investment. If Talent is not compensated differently, the inflationary model will grip the company, resulting in seasonal layoffs, lower profits, failures, or higher prices.

Recent articles have exposed the enormous sums of money compensating the heads of the major companies. Disney's calamities with payment to their chief executives and enormous parachutes also bring on an array of questions about what is just compensation. In baseball, the $25 million per year being paid to Alex Rodriguez has come under close scrutiny, especially in light of the collapse of the Texas Rangers who pay it. Most headlines are grabbed at the CEO level, and most compensation is going to that level, whether the CEO is a Talent or not. Under what circumstances is agreeing to a golden parachute an intelligent business decision?

Clearly, most people are not paid what they contribute to a corporation. Corporations have costs other than salaries, benefits, and travel expenses. Overhead, profits, plant, and many other costs associated with a corporation factor in. Some corporations derive their revenues and most of their activities from people, for example, a consulting company. Others are so highly automated that they need very few employees to generate large sales volumes. Clearly, most companies fall somewhere in between. Most have little idea what most of their employees contribute. Hiring decisions are made based on need and the grade level of the employee needed. The actual contribution of the employee is unknown but is expected to be above some minimum guidelines. For instance, the new employee might be required to generate sales in excess of ten times salary. Managers often hear employees complain that they should receive what they deliver to the company. They are partly right. They should receive compensation in line with the company's return on investment in them. I call that "return on Talent," and I dedicate a full chapter in this book to defining return on Talent and how to measure it. Practically speaking, it would be impossible to measure every employee's return on Talent. You need to choose wisely those people whom you believe to be talented and evaluate their impact to make sure they are being compensated properly.

What Do We Mean by "Talents"?

Talents are the relatively few people who contribute the most to the organization who need to be recognized, nurtured, and leveraged to maximize the positive results only they can achieve. They are different. They are the stars, and they need to be treated like stars. They contribute more and need to be compensated more than the knowledge workers. The notions of giving "pay for performance" and identifying exceptional contributors as "high-potential" employees (hi-pos) are not new. Indeed, they are common practice. Many corporations have been trying to manage the challenges of identifying the strongest contributors and treating them differently without creating excessive discontent in the rest of the workforce.

Corporations need to learn to deal with free agency without going broke by treating employees as customers. After all, as a hiring manager, you are trying to get Talent to buy what you are offering and then to develop loyalty with ongoing customer care to retain Talent. And just as corporations are increasingly segmenting high-valued customers for special attention, perhaps it is time to segment high-valued employees (customers) for special treatment.

Compensation should not be assumed as the primary factor in attracting and retaining Talent. Money is a big factor for some, but not for others. Talents have visions, purposes, and values. Coworkers, bosses, daily work environment, and opportunity to make big differences and to win at the game of business attract Talents as much or more than does money. Fair compensation is certainly a maintenance factor. Inadequate compensation is a disincentive. Excessive compensation does not guarantee happiness of Talent. The joy of work is a central factor in the productivity and satisfaction of Talents, and indeed of all workers from top to bottom in any organization.

Why This Book?

This book will:

- Help you see why you must treat Talent differently from most knowledge workers

- Tell how to measure return on Talent (ROT)

- Show how to maximize yourself and others as Talent

- Provide key elements of a Talent-friendly organization

- Suggest what is needed to attract, hire, keep, and best utilize Talent

- Tell how to leverage the Talent on your team

- Reveal the seven secrets of Talent

1 The Talent Value Chain

We are living in a time when talented people — many of them represented by powerful agents, attorneys, professional associations, or unions — dominate in business, as they have for the past four decades in athletics and entertainment.

In effect, all employees now can be classified as free agents and all fields of labor as performing arts — places where field performance (not politics, popularity, personality, potential, academic degrees, or social pedigrees) matters most, where the value a person adds on the job is recognized and rewarded, where managers and administrators serve as coaches and counselors and either become world-class leaders of talented people or lose their jobs.

For the first time at many business schools, M.B.A. graduates are choosing "talent tracks," performance fields, and entrepreneurial ventures over management positions in large organizations, having witnessed the mass exodus of many managers in merged and downsized companies.

We live in a talent economy. Today's economy is "ideacentric" and talent driven. Good ideas give birth to good products. Innovative ideas are driving the economy, creating wealth, and making people rich. More important, some bold ideas are changing the world for the better.

Providing a climate where people feel free and motivated to cultivate and implement constructive ideas is the challenge of talented leaders. Those who succeed in selling good ideas to others win financially, gain power, and assume a leadership role. Indeed, the only sustainable form of leadership is thought leadership — generating innovative ideas and making market adjustments faster than the competition. Even though the bubble of instant "dot-com" billionaires has burst, we have all been struck by the blinding light of the lasting truth: We live in the age of ideas, and the talented person who generates, implements, and successfully markets those innovative ideas wins exponentially more money, visibility, and credibility.

What every manager wants from a Talent is value-added contribution. But few managers know how to achieve this aim. To explain how to achieve this aim, I present in this chapter the Talent value chain.

Talent Breeds Innovation

Every successful innovation starts with imagination and knowledge.

Imagination + Knowledge = Innovation

The imagination and knowledge of talented people breed innovation. Places of innovation are where all talented people want to work — and imagination and knowledge pave the way.

The great scientist Albert Einstein said, "Imagination is more powerful than knowledge." Many of Einstein's theories in his later life are based on his own imagination. He never wrote "proof" of those theories. Scientists are still trying to prove some of them.

Knowledge can be acquired through reading, learning, and doing. But imagination must be cultivated and applied by each individual Talent. Every innovation starts in someone's imagination.

Walt Disney exercised his imagination in creating a fantasy land for kids regardless of cultural or language differences. If people come to Disneyland from Vietnam, South Africa, or India, without speaking any English, these people still enjoy Disneyland. By the end of the day their kids are excited and thankful for so much pleasure. There are no cultural boundaries or language barriers. That is the phenomenal power of the imagination.

Henry Ford mixed imagination with knowledge. He believed that one day every American family would own a car. And he had this belief when there were no paved highways.

Bill Gates, similarly, believed that every American family would want and need a personal computer. "Computers will do micro-surgery within the next 20 years," he predicts. If someone cannot imagine this in the first place, how is it going to happen?

Michael Dell can boast that only one company in the world increased its earnings and revenues at about 80 percent during its first eight years and at 55 percent per year for the next six years — and that was his company, Dell Computer Corporation. He achieved this by avoiding "traditional business thinking" and dealing directly with customers.

We are entering the age of excellence, an age with no geographic boundaries. In this age, every individual, organization, product, and service faces tremendous competition. To survive and grow, each individual and organization must keep improving. Mediocre work will not stand the test of time. Mediocre people, products, and organizations will suffer demise sooner or later. Only high-quality products, services, and strategies will guarantee survival and success. Where there is tremendous competition, you need to do something better and different.

CEO Michael Dell notes: "We surround ourselves with the best talent we can find and structure our business for success, even to the point of dividing up people's jobs. This has now become part of our culture. The first time we did it, some people said, 'You're cutting my job in half.' Six months later, because of growth, their job is the same size it was before, and they say, 'Please cut my job in half again.' We grow our business by dividing and conquering different parts of the market, which also helps us acquire new talent."

Five Links in the Idea-Talent Chain

When we see a good idea from its genesis through to successful implementation, we create a chain of events. Everybody has a good idea, but few ideas are ever brought to fruition. So, what chain of events has to happen?

1. Anticipation

Anyone who wants to win in the marketplace must anticipate the next wave and learn how not only to predict the next wave but also to create the next wave. With the intense competition we have now, people depend more upon innovative ideas — ideas that anticipate the next wave, start a trend, or at least ride a wave started by someone else.

For example, Michael Dell reports: "We strive to anticipate key trends in our business to gain a greater share of a faster-growing market. The Internet is one example. We know that virtually everybody will be buying computers over the Internet in five years. We want to dominate that market and have a leadership position in sales of computers through this new distribution channel. We also look aggressively for add-on businesses. We focus on clearly connected businesses and services that our customers want, such as peripherals in software, integration services, and financial services."

2. Articulation

You may have a great idea, but if you can't articulate it and express it well to others, it will never see the light of day. Everyone knows of great products that have failed because the message was not right.

For example, during the past few years, many entrepreneurs failed because they failed to articulate their vision and mission to themselves or to others. They seemed to focus more on having a successful IPO than on building a business. They failed to develop and articulate their plans for success, and they ruthlessly failed their people.

3. Acceptance

After you come up with an idea, you have to make sure that the people who surround the idea will accept it and embrace it and cherish it. You may have the best idea, but if the people you depend on are not cherishing it, it is useless. If everyone in your environment embraces and cherishes the idea, then you can build a successful organization and win customers' hearts.

For example, when Jeff Bezos started Amazon.com, he made sure that all his people cherished the idea of selling books over the Internet for the first time. At the beginning, many people thought, "I'm not going to buy a book without touching it first." But millions of people are now doing it because somebody believed in the idea and led others to accept it and bring it into reality.

4. Action

Even your best ideas may be obsolete within months, not years. So hurry. Fast action is required. If you have a good idea, you need to turn that idea into a good product or good service. You have to take the idea and make something out of it. Taking "action on time" is an important characteristic of successful entrepreneurs. With the advent of new technology and the growth of information technology and global competition, to become first you have to act fast. Speed is a vital factor in today's success. New products and new strategies emerge almost daily.

For example, hundreds of dot-com companies around the globe are trying to copy eBay's success on the auction business; virtually none is successful. Chrysler's PT Cruiser and 3M's Palm Pilot are still the leaders in their product lines due to "action on time." Many companies may try to copy them, but none has had similar success. The most important step that successful leaders take is "action on time." It is also the step where most ideas die. Almost everyone has good ideas, but how many are acted upon? Commitment to fast action is the key to success.

Proactive actions characterize market leaders. Michael Dell comments: "We've learned that we can't just follow the other guys. That approach won't create a lot of value. We try to find our own way and do things better. We may borrow good ideas from other companies when we see them, but we're not held to convention — and we're not striving to be like other companies. We're not trying to remake our company or merge with other firms so that we can have a different profile. We are building our own path."

5. Leverage

The fifth link is leverage. Leverage the idea, capture market share, and create wealth. The team who surrounds the individual Talent must leverage the idea into something much bigger. Together they enlarge the scope and scale by leveraging the idea through alliances and other means.

As Michael Dell comments: "We will continue to grow our business. Along with our talented team of employees, we plan to take the company to its full potential — for our customers, shareholders, and employees — for years to come."

Talent drives this chain of events to turn good ideas into reality. The combination of these five links yields the innovative product. Ideas die anywhere on this chain if there is not commitment to the idea.

Five Ways to Create Value

As Talent, you can create value in five ways, discussed in the following sections.

Make Sure Your Idea Is Unique, Authentic, and Genuine

Explore the genuineness before you implement the idea. You may have a phenomenal idea, but you don't know whether somebody has already done it or not. For example, when Amazon.com came up with the idea to sell books over the Internet, Barnes & Noble and Borders thought, "This is a good idea." So, they started BN.com and Borders.com. They have had some success but not even close to that of Amazon.

Expose the Idea to the Right People and Involve Those People Intensely

If you have a phenomenal idea, you have to select and involve the right people intensely in implementing your idea. You may need financial help to carry the idea off. You may need the endorsement of key players in the industry, or you may need to gather customers. Regardless, you want influential people to back your idea and a passionate team to implement it.

Ensure That All Information Is Adequate, Accurate, and Free Flowing at All Levels

Management should create an atmosphere that ensures that adequate and accurate information flows freely and fearlessly up, down, and sideways to facilitate the implementation of ideas. If information is held back, or there is lack of commitment, or misunderstandings of goals, then the project will fail.

Provide the Right Resources to People Involved

You may have a phenomenal idea, but if you cannot provide the right resources to the right people, then your idea will never be implemented. Provide the resources to make the product or service the best it can be. Don't take shortcuts that sacrifice a passion for excellence in order to save a few bucks.

Expect Something Unexpected; Many Failures, Surprises, and Setbacks Will Come, So Learn from These

"To invent something, you need a good imagination and a pile of junk," said Thomas Edison. It took Edison thousands of tries to get the electric light bulb to work. He knew that he would get it if he persevered. The movie *Titanic* was far behind schedule and incredibly over budget. If it had flopped at the box office, Viacom would have been headed for disaster. But Viacom managed to do it right; the rest is history.

The IDEA Value Cycle

On a personal level, gaining self-knowledge and self-confidence is vital to creating value. The "IDEA value cycle" can be spelled out as follows.

I—Invest in Yourself

Determination must be the first impulse toward becoming successful. Before you can find anything, you must find yourself. Soar on your strengths and contain your weaknesses until you can transform them into new strengths. Seek perfection — zero defects — in the product or process by fostering a zero defect philosophy in your people. Invest in them and help them to invest in themselves to gain the self-knowledge and self-confidence needed to help you win. Without investing wisely and regularly in Talent, you can't have great returns.

D—Different Thinking

In the future, there will be tremendous competition for everything, and the only way you can compete is to do a different thing or do a common thing differently. The strong comeback of Apple Computer Company is mostly credited to its founder, Steve Jobs, who characterizes himself as well as his organization with a simple motto: "Think Different." None of the other computer manufacturers had ever thought about using multicolored plastic bodies for personal computers before Jobs's iMac. Its success is not necessarily due to the product innovation or better performance, but rather to the "think different" strategy. Using the same strategy, the United Kingdom's most admirable entrepreneur, Anita Roddick, built her cosmetics empire, The Body Shop. Roddick's bold declaration: "Small chest, flabby thighs, large hips, thick lips, BIG DEAL — love your body." Different thinking creates value for the organization and society. Cultivation of mind produces different thinking.

E—Emotional Commitment

Commitment with emotion is the key to any success. In India it is called *sadhana*. When the famous sitarist Ravi Shankar was learning sitar from his guru, he didn't leave his room for many days until he learned the basics. He devoted all his time to sitar. That takes emotional commitment. Throughout history, you see the greatest successes coming from those who exhibited undying commitment. Michael Dell, Bill Gates, and Anita Roddick are emotionally committed to their endeavors. Their emotional commitment has helped them succeed. They all love their work. They have their own mission and commitment. Rather than jumping into the dot-com frenzy, they focused on their own beliefs. They want to create organizations that will dominate the economic landscape. They are passionate about making a contribution to society and creating a business culture of enlightenment. They want to create and deliver real value to their customers and shareholders. They have a "love it or leave it" philosophy. They don't do things only because they want to hit revenue numbers; rather, they "just do it" because they have emotional commitment. Michael Dell had a dream to beat IBM while IBM was the giant in the computer market. He succeeded by making the dream come true through his own emotional commitment.

The success of General Electric (GE) is largely credited to retired CEO Jack Welch's leadership in creating an "emotional bond" with employees. GE's Six Sigma initiative is not just a CEO-driven quality initiative. It is a management philosophy from top to bottom. Everyone is learning the same language of Six Sigma's revolutionary five-step process: define, measure, analyze, improve, and control (DMAIC). This philosophy creates an emotional bond among employees. And the results show it: GE reported record results; 2000 earning per share $1.27, up 19 percent; 2000 revenues grew 16 percent to $130 billion; earnings up 19 percent to $12.7 billion. Welch reported: "GE's double-digit increases in 2000 demonstrate the benefits of the company's emphasis on globalization, growth in services, Six Sigma quality, and e-Business."

Emotional commitment makes the difference between workers and fighters. Workers are typical 8-to-5 performers; fighters are reaching for excellence. They want to be winners in everything they do, whereas workers may not have that winning mentality. Workers are contractually obligated to do their jobs; fighters are mentally obligated. Fighters are risk takers, whereas workers are risk adverse. Above all, fighters are always emotionally committed.

Most workers don't have a winning mentality because they don't have a sense of ownership. If you own something, then you don't want to lose it. Profit sharing, reward, recognition, and bonuses are key ingredients to seed ownership within workers. In GE's Six Sigma initiative, "black belts" receive rewards for completing projects successfully and saving GE's bottom line. Contrast this level of commitment with that of many failed dot-coms whose owners admitted to starting a business just to go public or to be bought out.

A—Action

The most important thing that successful entrepreneurs do is take "action on time," as mentioned earlier. The attitude of "Just do it"—the slogan of Nike's founder and chairman, Phil Knight—is necessary for any success. If you have a bright idea, you must act on it; otherwise, someone else will eat your lunch. If you are not an implementer, find a partner who is.

Michael Dell notes: "A lot of favorable economics occur when you take time out of the process. Dell's model has about eight days of inventory. One competitor has 81 days of inventory and 40 more days of inventory in their distribution channel—16 weeks more than our eight days. A competitor with that level of inventory can't compete with Dell and make any money doing it. As a result, our business is growing fast, and our profitability exceeds that of all of our major competitors combined."

The action at Dell is centered on customers, as Michael Dell reports:

> We maintain an intense focus on the customer, even as we grow. Today, Dell is still ranked number one in customer satisfaction surveys. Our account teams work face-to-face with all of our large customers. We work with our suppliers to deliver materials on a pull basis. Instead of waiting to build a machine until we have all the materials in the warehouse, and then guessing what people will buy, we focus on how fast the inventory is moving. If we can shorten that time, not only will

we save our customers a lot of money, but also they'll get a superior product that meets their precise requirements.

The next frontier of competition is in the area of customer service quality. We're constantly looking for breakthroughs, such as our direct business model, that change the dynamics of the game. Finding a new way to deliver a better customer experience and more value at less cost is a good strategy.

By following the Talent value chain, you, too, can deliver a better experience for employees, customers, and all other stakeholders.

Although Dell admits making mistakes, we learned from them. We've developed overly ambitious products that tried to do everything for everybody—without a focus, they were bound to fail. The answer is not having a brilliant conception of all the best ideas before you start, but rather learning from your mistakes and not repeating them—and making sure that those lessons are passed along. As Dell states:

"There is such a thing as excessive growth that is not only too fast but dangerous. We grew in one year from $890 million in sales to $2.1 billion in sales. It was exciting, but one year later we hit the wall. We had to learn how to understand the profitability of different parts of our business, where our business was succeeding and where it wasn't, and how to anticipate and build an infrastructure to support growth.

When we had to focus on our best opportunities, we adopted the idea that return on invested capital was a great way to measure different parts of our business. If the cost of capital is about 15 percent and a business is earning 20 percent return on invested capital, it is creating value for shareholders.

By segmenting our business, we found the path to grow into an organization that has many different businesses. We have a business selling to large customers, to global customers, to the consumer. And these businesses have different characteristics. You separate those, and you create management opportunities. This approach allows us not only to aggressively bring Talent into the company and grow Talent, but also to get very finely focused on the unique needs of specialized customers and achieve high returns on invested capital."

2 Winning the Creative War

In the first chapter, we learned that modern societies are driven by innovative ideas and that these ideas are based on creativity and imagination. In this chapter, I explain the creative war or the so-called war for Talent and suggest the implications. I explain the war for Talent in terms of the creativity and obsolescence cycle and suggest that to survive in an environment of competition, you need to engage in the continuous development cycle and the on-time obsolescence cycle.

Talent and Environment

To innovate, organizations must emphasize two things: Talent and environment.

An organization has to employ and retain the best, brightest, and most diversified people in order to innovate. The aim is to create what I call a united talent workforce. You want people who will work together to bring out better products faster. You need to provide Talent with appropriate resources for innovation. Following their initial success, Talents must adopt this philosophy: "Change a goal; change a habit; change a mind." Talents have to change their goals, habit patterns, and mind-sets to focus on the next success.

You should create and keep a constant learning environment — an entrepreneurial environment that fosters creativity. Create a fearless environment where people can dialog and collaborate with one another. Create a diversified environment where different people think differently and value each other's thinking. Create new ways of looking at problems and opportunities and a strong sense of urgency. Create a culture that effectively leverages Talent.

Winning by Leveraging Talent

Whether leading or lagging, in long races, those who go fastest win. As GE's Jack Welch said in many different ways, the only sustainable competitive advantage is to innovate and change faster than the toughest competitors. He also emphasized that if the outside is changing faster than you are, the end is in sight. In business, just as in racing, those who go fastest have the combination of the fastest vehicle and the most talented driver. And the fastest vehicle was created by the most talented group of designers, engineers, and fabricators, a winning mix of talented leaders and a strong cast of highly motivated, hard-working doers. The talented driver is the manager-leader who maintains the winning combination of continuous development and on-time obsolescence.

Business is no more than the extension of its key Talent in the value chain. That's why, over the past two decades, the emphasis in business has shifted from maintenance to meaning, from putting in time to making a contribution, from politics to value-added performance, from labor to talent.

In the business context, *Talent* may be defined as "capability applied to create value that is recognized and rewarded by primary stakeholders — owners, managers, and customers." Talented people must know how their jobs fit within the value chain and not only perform the routine tasks well but also excel at the high-leverage components of their jobs.

The high-leverage components usually require some degree of proactivity, creativity, initiative, and ingenuity. If talented people are not regularly operating at the high end of their jobs and being leveraged wisely by management, most of their talent is wasted. In fact, talent is wasted whenever it is not recognized, developed, expressed, refined, and leveraged.

Now let me define what I meant by "value chain." A value chain connects customers with creators, giving customers the impression (or illusion) of intimacy and identity with the organization and supplying them with the value they want and need to return again and again. In a product-based business, the value chain may have these ten links:

1. creative ideas

2. constructive criticism

3. concept development

4. testing-feedback

5. finished product

6. packaging-marketing

7. sales

8.   support-service

9.   management systems-processes

10. leadership

Every business needs top Talent at every link because the business will be only as strong as its weakest link. Moreover, the Talent at every vital link must feel valued. To the extent that Talents feel like victims, performance suffers proportionately.

What talent matters most in your business? Every member of the value chain matters to the customer. Leaders should recognize that the new definitions of talent and value do not exclude any member of the organization. All employees should feel, as should all members of an athletic team, that they play a vital role and might, through diligence and intelligent application of talent, become indispensable (in a here-and-now business sense). This means that on any given day, or on any given shift, their presence and performance not only "matter," but also make all the difference in the world.

I think every person likes the feeling of being a "count-on-me" Talent. But people may not stay happy in the system if, after proving themselves, they aren't recognized and rewarded.

How is Talent best recognized and rewarded? No one way suits all. To the extent possible, rewards should be personalized, based on the preferences and priorities of each individual Talent. Is this too much to ask, you say? Not if you want to be a market leader. The size of the operation is not the critical factor; the critical factor is the habit of showing appreciation.

How is top Talent best recruited? Top-performing environments attract top Talent. The best Talents flow to the best companies to work for. These performers may be influenced by colleagues, peers, and media polls; a lot of recruitment happens by word of mouth in every industry. Talents seek creative freedom, expression, performance options, growth, and a supportive environment with capable owners, managers, coaches, cheerleaders, team members, and pay-for-performance systems.

How is top Talent best retained? In retaining Talent, common sense is not common practice. It is easy to cite factors such as a winning program, achievement, stability in the front office, relationship of trust with ownership, collegiality with colleagues, awards, recognition, growth, learning, and money. But personalities and politics complicate matters. Also, top Talents, especially when represented by top agents and attorneys, often become their own worst enemies by expecting and demanding too much.

How is Talent best leveraged? I see seven ways:

1.   Teams. Put top Talent with other top Talent in teams and give them challenging and meaningful work to do. Make sure this work is valued by the organization and its customers.

2.   Special projects. There's nothing quite like a special assignment, some "mission impossible" or high-priority project, to bring out the best in Talent.

3.   Products. Pour top Talent into products that can be replicated and widely distributed. By creating new products and improving existing products, you gain immense leverage.

4.   Distribution. Seek wide distribution for the work of top Talent. If the world-class work of your top Talent is poorly promoted and distributed, you gain little leverage.

5.   Marketing-sales. Leverage Talent through marketing and sales events. This may mean featuring Talents in ads or involving them in sales in some way.

6. Advertising-public relations. Make your top Talents bigger than life. Create an image and identity for them. Invest wisely in advertising and public and media relations to make a brand of the Talents' names.

7. Mentoring-modeling-coaching. Engage willing, mature Talent in the high-leverage activities of mentoring, modeling, and coaching new Talent.

What is the new role of managers and leaders? Like management in the sports and entertainment worlds, the primary role of management in business is to support, serve, discipline, and leverage Talent. The leader often asks four questions: How is it going? What are you learning? What are your goals now in light of how it is going and what you are learning? How can I help you? In this way, the leader avoids owning the problem and yet offers himself or herself as a source of help. The leader's responsibility is to create conditions of trust, set up performance agreements, allow people to perform, and then hold people accountable — all with the aim of being competitive and making a greater contribution to society.

Talent to Meet the Competition

In this borderless era, each individual, organization, product, and service faces tremendous competition from inside and outside home countries. Once while I was visiting a U.S. automaker assembly plant, I asked a group of workers, "What does the word *globalization* mean to you?" Most defined *globalization* in terms of the prospect of losing their jobs as a result of rising competition.

Intraindustrial competition is competition within the same group of industries, such as General Motors competing with Toyota or Ford. Fierce competition leads organizations to merge with each other.

Interindustrial competition is competition within different industries. For example, Microsoft is a leader in PC software business, but it sells cars through its Microsoft car point website. Who would have thought that Microsoft would be selling cars? Similarly, Amazon.com is selling more than books these days over the Internet. If you look at its website, you see that Amazon.com primarily sells books. That is what it is known for. But now it is competing not just with leading book retailers such as Barnes & Noble and Borders. Amazon has entered the auction business to compete against eBay.

Interindustrial competition is bringing together companies from different industries. As mergers among organizations in one industry phase out, mergers will increase among organizations in other industries as organizations seek competitive advantage.

Mergers, reconstructions, and expansions of business are responses to competition, challenges, globalization, and technological advancements. Perhaps one reason why the pace of mergers and acquisitions has slowed in recent months is that on average, three of every four mergers disappoint shareholders. According to a November 2000 study by leading consulting firm KPMG, "83 percent of the 700 largest corporate mergers fail to boost the stock price because of poor execution." Merger does not mean monopoly. Some deals pay off, but many don't — precisely because the managements of both companies often lose sight of the prime importance of key Talent.

AOL Time Warner. Gerald M. Levin, CEO of Time Warner, announced in January 2000 that he was selling Time Warner to America Online in an unprecedented deal marrying old and new economy forces. Digital will prevail over analog, new media will grow faster than the old, and those businesses that can effectively combine the Internet with the traditional business will become the twenty-first-century establishments. In the AOL–Time Warner merger, Stephen M. Case, chairman of AOL Time Warner, is betting that by merging the Time Warner colossus with his Internet empire, he will create a hybrid with unmatched advantages when the long-anticipated convergence of entertainment, information, communications, and online services occurs in the next few years. But this can happen only if both companies take care of their Talent.

Chase Manhattan Corp. and J. P. Morgan and Co. This merger combined $670 billion in assets. Such megamergers are pairing investment banks with commercial banks, brokerages, and market makers. But returns to shareholders of merged companies lag behind industry averages.

Daimler-Chrysler. This is an example of a merger that was like mixing oil and water — the cultures of the two companies have clashed. So far, Daimler-Benz's $36 billion takeover of Chrysler Corp. is a challenge for all.

AT&T's back-to-back deal with TCI and Mediaone. This deal had a combined worth of $90 billion, but it backfired on CEO C. Michael Armstrong. He tried to sell consumers on packaged telecom services, but AT&T's business slowed considerably.

Talent Is Key in Mergers

Most managers think about a merger in accounting terms, not in terms of how to make the merger better for the stakeholders of the companies. When you merge two companies, you create a totally different entity. To make a merger or acquisition effective, managers should focus on four issues.

Talent

Locate the Talents in the two organizations and put them in key positions to make sure the merger goes according to plan. As long as there is unbridled competition, each individual and organization must struggle to survive. But struggle is good for individuals and organizations because it builds competitive strength. Escapism is not good for the organization or its members. An organization's success depends on the fighting spirit of its talented men and women.

Culture

In any merger there is always a collision of culture. To minimize the damage, managers need to identify the culture of each organization, measure the cultural gap between the merging organizations, analyze the cultural-business barriers, and remove these barriers.

Single Vision, Not Double Vision

When two companies with two different visions merge, they may still go in two different directions with two different visions. To avoid double vision and have a strong single vision, managers need to clearly understand the business, establish financial targets, set time lines, create a deployment plan, provide sufficient resources, assign accountability, and continuously communicate progress.

Performance

To improve performance in the merged company, managers need to measure short-term and long-term performances, analyze the performances, and improve the performances by engaging in the build-and-rebuild cycle.

Throughout history, we see that one generation often struggles mightily to establish the nation, the second generation struggles to grow the nation, and the third generation struggles to maintain the status quo and harvest the fruit from the work of their ancestors. Within three generations, the build-and-maintain cycle shifts gradually toward the build-and-rebuild cycle. Similarly, only the fittest, finest, best organizations survive. Excellence succeeds. Every day you have to rebuild your strategy, products, and services. You have to constantly change. You have to build something new or better.

General Electric. Jack Welch helped make General Electric one of America's most admired and profitable companies. He had a build-and-rebuild style with people, assets, and strategies. He became known as "Neutron Jack" because of his early decision to downsize 100,000 people. He then became one of the most successful and admired CEOs for transforming GE and delivering profits consistently for twenty years. He practiced a continuous build-and-rebuild cycle rather than a build-and-maintain cycle. If Jeffrey R. Immelt, Welch's successor as CEO of GE, only imitates Jack Welch's style with people, assets, and strategies, he will not be as successful. Immelt must create his own style and strategy. Often a new CEO comes in and tries to maintain the same model but fails to get similar results.

Montgomery Ward. Think about the crash of Montgomery Ward, a 128-year-old department store chain. It was extremely creative in the 1960s and 1970s, but, in the 1990s, it fell back to a build-and-maintain model. The competition — Sears and others — was using a build-and-rebuild model. And so we witnessed the collapse of an American retailing icon.

Microsoft. Bill Gates had what amounted to a monopoly, and then the Internet helped level the playing field. Perhaps Gates was a bit shocked that some upstarts came in and beat Microsoft at its own game. But that's what Netscape did. It was building while Microsoft was maintaining. To shock his employees out of complacency, Gates told them, "We are going out of business. Could you please save us?" This might sound amusing coming from one of the world's richest persons. But Gates meant it. His sense of urgency is the key to a turnaround. He has the determination and dedication to do something better.

Continuous Development Cycle

Growth and progress depend on a continuous development cycle (CDC). A CDC has two stages. The first stage is the discovery stage — the innovation of new products and services. The second stage is the maturity stage. It brings mature, defect-free products or services into the market. The first stage creates, and the second stage improves. The typical product cycle has four phases — infant, young, adult, and old (see figure 2-1). The leading product cycle has only two phases — infant and young. The discovery stage leads to the infant phase. The improvement stage extends throughout the four phases of the product life cycle. Typically, financial growth increases through the young phase, then gradually declines and ul-

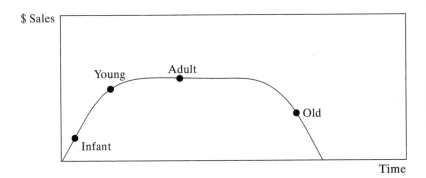

Figure 2-1 **Product life cycle chart**

timately dies out. So, as painful as it is, you may have to kill your product and replace it before it transforms from young to adult in order for you to be a market leader. Market leaders introduce new products before existing products reach the old phase.

With the advancement of technology, competition, and globalization, the life cycle phases of products continue to shrink. In years past, when a product was introduced into the market, it survived for a long time. Now, more products with short life spans are being developed as distribution channels and rapid information dispersion allow for rapid delivery and obsolescence. For example, think about the PC revolution. In the 1980s buying a computer every five years was a luxury. Now every year many consumers demand faster and better computers. So as organizations create and introduce more products faster, the life cycle phases of products become shorter.

The Discovery Stage Is Revolutionary

The discovery stage is revolutionary because it creates something new. It is where ideas are created and applied. It is the stage where Talent shines. Most truly revolutionary products and services are seeded by the ideas of one individual, a Talent. Organizations need a discovery stage in each sector of products, services, strategy, and marketing. And organizations need Talents in the discovery stage to win the competitive war. In today's environment of rapid, short life cycles, the organization with the most new products and services wins. When an organization introduces a product into the market, the organization may enjoy a temporary monopoly — until others enter the market. Growth occurs because of the introduction of the new product. Sales grow rapidly during the first few years of introduction. In a leading company, a vast majority of its current products were introduced within the last two or three years. This type of dynamic marketplace puts a premium on Talent. This is why corporations are scrambling to attract and keep talent — more and better Talent than their toughest competitor has.

For example, the introduction of **Intel**'s 80X86 processor used in the IBM PC was revolutionary. The processor delivered more performance and a platform that corporations and individuals would come to use. Intel continued to innovate in releases such as the Pentium I, but the changes were evolutionary. When Intel introduced the PC processor, it was revolutionary. An incredible industry was established. When the Pentium was introduced as a successful evolution of the product, there was continued excitement. New products and services drive business growth and health. Talents are the drivers of new products and services. Competition for Talent is becoming as fierce as competition for customers.

The introduction of **television** in the 1950s was revolutionary, and then the introduction of multichannel cable TV forty years later was evolutionary. When the television was introduced for the first time in a box, people were genuinely excited. Color was the next major improvement. Cable followed without much excitement but certainly with winning results.

The introduction of the **Internet** was revolutionary, even though the connection speed was very slow compared to that of today. Now enhancements happen almost daily, but still that initial excitement you felt when you first made Internet connections and communicated with your friends all over the world by e-mail can never be replicated.

When the **Palm Pilot** came out, it created a level of excitement that was simply not there for its predecessors. It was revolutionary. It created great excitement because it brought a new product to consumers with a message that they could buy into. There were other handhelds before the Palm. The Palm Pilot was a mixture of maturing technology and better marketing. It is a good example of taking an idea and making it marketable. The Palm Pilot is still the market leader in its product category.

When **Apple Computer** introduced the mouse, customers embraced Apple computers. The mouse was developed at Xerox, and the first commercial implementation of the mouse was on the Apple Lisa, but then the Lisa failed. It was not until the Mac was released that the mouse succeeded. Apple did extremely well for several years. But in the late 1990s Apple's sales dropped, and its stock price plunged rapidly. What did Apple do? It brought back the Talent that had first made it successful — Steve Jobs. And what did Steve Jobs do? Introduce new colors to Apple computers. Consumers fell in love with those colorful computers. Within a year Apple's stock quadrupled. The innovation wasn't revolutionary from a technology perspective, but evolutionary innovation was perceived as revolutionary and exciting by customers. Without Steve Jobs's talent, Apple might not have survived.

The Maturity Stage Is Evolutionary

The challenges in the maturity stage are different from but just as demanding as those in the discovery stage. For example, it is not that unusual to find defects or problems in new product introductions. Some corporations need some time to perfect the design of their new product. Other corporations with great talent are able to introduce new products with almost no early problems. They win over the long term with consistently higher-quality and more-reliable products and services.

Another example is new models of cars. They are often much better a few years after the initial launch when the bugs have been worked out. After introducing a new model, an automaker wants to fix the problems identified in customer complaints in the model's later years. In this way, a product gradually improves. The leading companies have far fewer problems with new product introductions. As a result, they enjoy year-over-year gains in market share. Those that let customers fix their problems are in dire need of Talents who can help get products and services right before they get to customers. Using customer complaints to guide design of a product is rather pitiful.

Advanced CDC

Organizations must follow the CDC to grow. Most organizations follow one stage at a time. But to become market leaders, organizations must start a new discovery stage before they finish the maturity stage. To keep up with the competition and technological advancement, organizations need to reinvent their products regularly. Without a constant flow of CDC, a business is condemned to obsolescence.

This is perhaps best illustrated in the drug industry. Because of trademark issues, drug companies must innovate before competitors are allowed to create generic drugs. In this industry, you innovate or die.

Soft drink manufacturer Snapple CEO Michael Weinstein, who turned that company around, said: "We're not in the soft drink business; we are in the fashion business. It is a constant whirl of new products, flavors and packaging, pitched to consumers who want the latest thing."

Computer software companies are also in a constant whirl of new products and midlife kickers for existing products. The computer software industry cannot survive without CDC. For example, if Microsoft had stuck with its Windows operating system version 3.1, Microsoft could never have become the PC operating systems leader. What if Microsoft had taken this attitude: "We have all the market share in Windows, so why modify version 3.1? We sold millions of copies around the world, so let us enjoy the good life."? Microsoft did not take that attitude. Rather, it recognized that Windows 3.1 was just a start. In 1995, it introduced Windows 95. Then it introduced Windows 98, and then Windows Millennium edition. Why? Because the same buyers are coming back for upgrades.

Similarly, high tech hardware companies are in a constant whirl of new products. For example, do you need Intel's Pentium IV? You may tell me that you are very happy with Pentium II or Pentium III. But, in two years you will likely be using a Pentium IV or better. And you'll say, "After six months, the price dropped, and so I bought it." You take advantage of the upgrade.

On-Time Obsolescence

In a typical product sales curve, sales go up, level off, and then head down. When sales are flattening, you introduce the new product, and it starts its uphill climb, which will generally be faster than the first. During this time, while the first is hanging on and the new is growing fast, you get rapid growth (figure 2-2) as opposed to the growth you get by waiting (figure 2-3). By knowing your attrition rate, you can plan for new releases or new products to give you the growth rate you want.

For example, most book publishers know that their backlist (books over one year old) will retain their sales at a certain rate (say, about 70 percent) because the backlist attrition rate for books one year old varies little over time. So, publishers know they would need to get about half of last year's sales this year in new products to get a 20 percent increase. They plan for revisions when they see a title showing signs of downward movement. There is always risk in introducing new products. Some books go on for years selling at the same level, so a publisher could be hurt by revising too early.

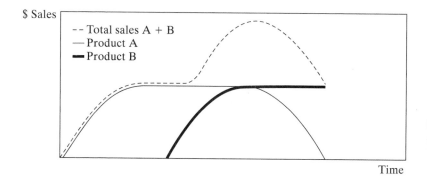

Figure 2-2 On-time obsolescence cycle

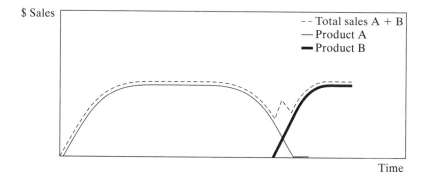

Figure 2-3 Traditional obsolescence cycle

The rate at which the old product falls off is critical to growth. You want your old product hanging on while your new one is in growth mode. Many people make the mistake of killing their best products too soon. Many market leaders kill their products before they die a natural death. Obsolescence creates value-added de-

mand. Obsolescence pushes out the old and creates new. It breaks
the monotony. On-time obsolescence brings out a better and unique
version of an existing product when your competitor just entered
the same market. The rate of decline decides if and when you kill
the product.

Invoking on-time obsolescence means you have to introduce
new products and improve old products constantly. You cannot celebrate for long. In today's environment, you have to innovate with
new products constantly to stay ahead.

In the infant phase of the product life cycle, you think about
growth. For example, in the infant and young phases of the Palm
Pilot, the organization made a lot of money and grew. When Palm
Pilot came to the adult phase, growth peaked, and then it slowed.
But 3Com was already thinking about Palm2 and Palm3. Research
continues. By the time one model reaches the adult phase or competition comes in, 3Com introduces a new or updated product —
and that is why Palm became and remained a market leader.

Another example is Chrysler's PT Cruiser, one of the most successful new vehicles in recent automotive history. Consumer demand is still strong, and yet in January 2001, the *Detroit Free Press*
reported: "Even the red hot PT Cruiser will cool off if Chrysler is
content to watch sales roll in, rather than introduce new versions to
keep the vehicle's incredible buzz alive." Indeed, Chrysler was ill
prepared for the success of the PT Cruiser. It failed to manufacture
enough to come close to demand, losing tens of thousands of sales.
Its $5,000 fee above the retail price for Cruisers on "back order"
was an attempt to minimize the damage and get supply and demand in synchronization. This was a case where talented people in
the design area were able to come up with a revolutionary idea, but
the Talent necessary to get the job done on the manufacturing end
was not there. The designers are thinking out to 2004 and beyond,
already working on a new and improved model or another product

so that they can create another buzz. Who knows: There may not even be a PT Cruiser in four years.

Mature industries have a hard time with product and service innovation, but market leaders in mature industries show that it can be done. When Boeing, the world leader in aerospace, introduced the 747, the huge two-story plane, Boeing officials must have thought, "The 747 is such a big plane that nobody will ever want or need a bigger commercial passenger plane." Now, in a remarkably competitive gesture, last year Airbus introduced the A3XXX, a model that is bigger than the Boeing 747. In the first-class section, you can take a sauna bath or take advantage of a sleeping compartment.

Time to Market

The company that introduces the first product into a market often enjoys a temporary monopoly. "Time waits for no one," said Jeff Levy, founder and CEO of eHatchery, an Atlanta-based e-business incubator. "If you don't do it now, the opportunity will be gone forever." The e-business market has taught us this perhaps better than any other. Look at all the millionaires who were made in e-business because they were early. What are the chances today?

Make your own product the model for success. While others are building products that match up against your original product, you can leap ahead of them again. At the right time, you can introduce a new and better model of the old product, leaving your competition one step behind. If you can predict the perfect time to obsolete your product, you have a better shot at success. Today, two of the most crucial factors for success are time to launch and time to obsolescence. Speed is the competitive edge. Speed can be a key factor in successfully implementing new products and services. Speed enables on-time delivery, time to launch, and time to learn. But if you increase only speed, you may not win the game. You have to know when to start, when to stop, when and where to restart, when to launch a product, and when to obsolete a product. When you launch a product, you have to realize that its expected life span is short. The marketing window of opportunity may be closing. You need a flawless on-time strategy. Then increase the speed. For example, if you are planning to introduce a new cell phone, you have to think about what people will want next when you are ready to release the product to market and start working on that new concept.

Wayne Gretzky, the great hockey player, said, "I don't skate to where the puck is now but where it will be." If you introduce your new cell phone in May 2002, you may plan to obsolete it by May 2003 because the product may have peaked. And you need to have that new model or new feature ready by March 2003 so you don't lose momentum in the market.

3 Talent: Engine of the New Economy

The engine of the new economy must be the best engine if we are to get to the front and stay there. In order to create and keep improving the best engine more rapidly than the competition, we need the best team of Talents and implementers in the world. Anything short of a passion to be the best on the planet is a road to mediocrity and disappointment.

To create new products or processes, the masterminds will be a unique group of people. In this chapter I will discuss who are the Talents, the difference between Talents and knowledge workers, people quality management, and environment needs for a Talent to perform like a Talent.

Talent Creates

A Talent is a creator, a rule breaker, a rule maker, a change initiator, and a knowledge generator. Talents are the spirits of an enterprise. They open the door of knowledge to everyone. In an era of competition, the growth of any organization is proportional to the growth of its Talent.

Talents are an unbeatable breed. Talents, in broad terms, are always thinking about the next move, wanting to excel. They are never satisfied. Ideas become reality when a group of focused and motivated Talents work together to make it happen. Technology is changing dramatically and rapidly. Business models are changing constantly, making it difficult to run businesses profitably without the help of exceptional Talent. In every sector or division, organizations need creative and productive Talent to succeed. It is during times of change when Talents offer the most gain because they are the change agents.

Why do we need creative Talent? Talent innovates. Talent responds to an ever-changing business environment and competition. Talent can implement the right strategy at the right moment. Talent utilizes resources in a more efficient way to boost productivity. Talent has a winning mentality. Talent never wants to stop. Talent seeks the next achievement. Talent energizes her coworkers. Talent carries more responsibility for success and failure. Talent creates a sense of urgency. As product life cycles become shorter, the life span of a business depends more on Talents and their ability to drive innovations. The challenge is how to surround our workplace or community with Talent — to make every organization Talent centered.

Talented Leaders Win

Talented leaders multiply the wins for everyone involved with their organizations.

Sumner Redstone, CEO of Viacom and author of *A Passion to Win,* says: "I've always wanted to win. I think winning is everything. Throughout my life I've had an obsessive drive to be number one. That doesn't mean I've always been number one. But that's what drives me — a desire to be the best at what I do." He tells of the hotel fire in which he was badly burned — and then of being in the heat of negotiating and deal making — and yet at age seventy-eight of being in perfect health. "The question isn't whether you are subjected to adversity and conflict during your life," he says. "The question is how you deal with it. If you really want to succeed, you have to be passionate and have a commitment to excellence in performance. If you have both of those, and some intellectual capacity, nothing is impossible. Optimism is not optional in business — it's vital. I believe that optimism is the only philosophy of life that's compatible with sustained success and sanity. So if you want to stay sane, you have to be optimistic and have confidence in yourself and your team."

Redstone is known as the consummate champion of Talent and content. "I believe that talent is king because people don't watch TV, they watch talent, content, programming. The way you manage talent is to let them run their business to a large extent. If you have confidence in the talent of your managers, you do not intrude every time they make a decision."

Beyond capability in Talent, Redstone looks for character and loyalty. "I look for some one I can trust, and who trusts me. And, I look for confidence, competence, and commitment."

To maintain a culture of innovation and creativity at Viacom, Redstone cultivates creative Talent. "Where does great content come from? Creativity. And where does creativity come from? From people who work in creative environments and associate with creative leaders. We maintain a high degree of innovation and creativity because we also have a high degree of financial discipline — and one works right along side the other. But money is never the driver. Most talented people are not motivated primarily by money but by the desire to achieve, to win, to be the best, and to try to make a positive difference through their work every day. They have a sense of mission."

Redstone is a prime example as he continues to lead Viacom at age seventy-eight. "The word 'retirement' was somehow omitted from my dictionary. I love what I do. I'm surrounded by brilliant people, many of whom could run Viacom. I respect their views, and I want to hear them. If they disagree with me, I want to hear that too. And they don't hesitate to tell me. Naturally if they disagree, I want them to have some solid reasoning behind their position or point of view. But I respect and trust my team. I know I can trust them, and they know they can trust me. Mutual trust is the most important element in running a company. Without it, you lose. I would like to think that I'm making some kind of a dent in the universe for the better. I'm not sure that's the case. I know I try. And if you try, perhaps you succeed. But the best news is — I am not yet finished."

Bill Gates manages thousands of engineers who work for him to create better Windows operating systems and associated software. These people are mostly knowledge workers who understand computers, but they do little to innovate. These knowledge workers are really good at achieving tasks set out for them, but Talent innovates. Bill Gates is one of a kind. He thinks years ahead. His talent is creating value, tactics, and psychology. Some argue that Gates is just a brilliant tactician who freezes markets and innovation by announcing products long before they are ready. Then startup companies in the market have to fight it out in a market awaiting Microsoft. If they survive, their products are reproduced by Microsoft, and Microsoft can leverage its existing market position to destroy the competition.

Anita Roddick is the talented person who started The Body Shop and transformed retailing. Not only did she become one of Europe's most successful entrepreneurs, but also she is giving back to society. In her book, *Business as Unusual,* she shares her own life experiences. She talks about building partnerships, which is the key to the relationships with communities. Roddick states: "The relationship is not a hierarchy, where one gender or rank lords it over another, but a partnership of equals, where both sides can learn from each other. The relationship has to be a learning partnership too: each has to learn enough about the other to work with them effectively." Her organization, The Body Shop, took community partnerships further than other companies had dared to before — putting missing persons' pictures on its trucks and working with HIV-positive families.

John Chambers, CEO of Cisco Systems in San Jose, holds meetings with senior managers to convert knowledge workers to Talent. He tells new hires and acquisitions: "You have a chance to find something within Cisco that really turns you on. You have a chance to make a difference by making a major contribution. But, you have to take a lot of initiative to do that."

Michael Jordan, who is working with the Washington Wizards — one of the worst teams in the NBA — is trying to make them winners. He is making progress, but it is slow. Progress doesn't happen overnight. Michael Jordan is a very talented person. Nike redefined an industry with him. His attention to detail and level of commitment made him the greatest in the game.

Phil Jackson, coach of the champion Los Angeles Lakers, is a talented person. Although some people think Michael Jordan is why Jackson won six NBA championships in Chicago, you cannot consistently do something like that without being a Talent yourself. His talent is managing Talent. He made the Lakers champions, too. His unique style has made him probably the only coach who can handle Shaq and Kobe at the same time. Remember that he also handled Dennis Rodman.

These public figures are real Talents. They are wealthy, famous heroes in their fields. You may ask, "So, what do people like that have to do with me?" The answer is everything. Talent has no boundaries, no exclusions. Talent, real talent, resides in all walks of life on all continents around the planet. Talent is not reserved for the celebrities who started as unknown talented people. Their talent helped them transform themselves from ordinary to special. Some leverage their talent to reach the sky. Others let it slip away into the ordinary.

Seven Differences between Talents and Knowledge Workers

All Talents are knowledge workers, but not all knowledge workers are Talents. Talents are more than knowledge workers. To operate successfully, every organization needs both Talents and knowledge workers. Knowledge workers may become Talents through dedication and a well-defined goal, but most don't make the transformation. Here are seven differences between Talents and knowledge workers:

Talents Make and Break the Rules; Knowledge Workers Conserve the Rules
The main difference between Talents and knowledge workers is that Talents break the rules, create, initiate, invent, direct, send — Talents take initiative. They are proactive. Knowledge workers, in

general, do not. Knowledge workers take orders. They are studious and obedient people. Just because a person is brilliant or has a Ph.D. does not mean that person is talented. One need not be a genius to be a Talent.

In the 1950s, when Dr. W. Edwards Deming begged American companies to improve their quality they didn't listen. He continued to beg into the 1980s, when corporate America finally listened. Of course, by then Japan had a thirty-year head start, from which the Western world has never recovered. He made rule by incredible persistence a key characteristic of a Talent. His ideas provided a great service to society but were slow to gain acceptance in the Western world.

Breaking the rules is not necessarily the road to glory and wealth. The dot-bombs broke all the rules of business leadership. Many had no visible means of actually making money by offering something for sale. They simply sold their ideas to people with money who clearly did not use diligence in recognizing unrealistic business plans. They broke the rules and bombed out at the expense of many broken lives.

Talents Create; Knowledge Workers Implement

Talents are your ingenuity source. They are creative. But creative Talents need support from knowledge workers to make the products and services and get them to customers. For an example in a different arena, scientists are Talents who do research with the help of associates (knowledge workers). In business organizations, knowledge workers help Talents to transform ideas into reality.

Talents Initiate Change; Knowledge Workers Support Change

Talents can feel the need to initiate change before it becomes necessary to change. Talents generally initiate change within the organization. But Talents need visionary knowledge workers who support the change. Without the support of knowledge workers, it would not be possible for Talents to bring about the changes within the organization. Even the rare Talents who can intertwine Talent behaviors and knowledge worker behaviors as the circumstances demand need the support of additional knowledge workers to implement innovations and changes.

Talents Innovate; Knowledge Workers Learn

Talents innovate, and knowledge workers learn and apply those innovations in the organization. Talents are the teachers; knowledge workers are the good students. A Talent may create a programming language and teach it to the knowledge workers, and then knowledge workers would learn, use, and refine the language.

Talents Direct; Knowledge Workers Act

Talents direct knowledge workers to perform the work. Good knowledge workers learn to deal with the idiosyncrasies that seem to be characteristic of Talents. With the direction of Talents, knowledge workers perform their work. Knowledge workers carry out the visions and marching orders of Talents.

Talents Inspire and Lift People;
Knowledge Workers Receive Information and Motivation

If you are a talented person, you likely want to help the next generation; you want to lift the people who work around you; you want to see those people become successful. And yet when some of those people fail, you become frustrated. Knowledge workers don't understand this. Often knowledge workers don't understand what Talents are after because they are so different. Knowledge workers have to understand what Talents are after, what their missions are. Unfortunately, Talents are not always good at explaining their ideas and intents to their knowledge workers. No Talent is perfect.

Talents need to work on their weaknesses as they play to their strengths. If you are a talented manager, and you have ten knowledge workers reporting to you, you need to take time to get them to share the excitement of the dream with you. Show them your love for what you do and pass that ball to them.

Talents Make an Immense Contribution and Create Immense Wealth; Knowledge Workers Share

Talents create a lot of wealth, and a lot of people share in that wealth. But making lots of money is not what drives most Talents. Many of them are inspired to make a difference or contribute to society. Knowledge workers may not be Talents, but they share in the joy of work and the wealth that Talents create. And often, if knowledge workers stay long enough, they catch the spirit of what Talents have done and begin to share in creating value for other people. They may do that by working in their workplace, by volunteering, by coaching an athletic team, or by teaching at a school, but they find ways to do it.

How Can Knowledge Workers Become Talents?

What do you say to a manager who asks, "I have many workers working here. I see the difference now between knowledge workers and Talent. I want more Talent. How can I get more?" If you can give knowledge workers a fear-free environment, they might excel. Dr. Deming taught us to drive out fear. But only a few companies have no fear at all in their cultures.

As knowledge workers take more initiative, they can become Talents. Even if Talents can't influence the macroeconomic conditions in the environment, they can deeply influence those within their circle. They should ensure that those people who report to them or work with them have no fear to freely express their views. Most people have been taught to have fears. But you can teach them not to fear. For example, you can take the time to involve them in your projects. Often managers do not involve others. How often do you take the people who report to you on some learning adventure? At Cisco, CEO John Chambers takes all the people who report to him — his whole management team — with him to do some adventure together. Because of that shared experience, they don't have as much fear of each other. They courageously take action and express themselves.

Part of this conversion from knowledge worker to Talent depends on the depth and breadth of financial incentives and other motivations. Financial incentives are one reason why the Six Sigma quality initiatives became so successful at General Electric. Six Sigma initiatives may not be as successful in other organizations because at General Electric, if you do the work, you get rewarded. If you are a "black belt" and save or make the company $1 million on a project, you get a percentage of that.

Incentives encourage Talents to break the rules, create, initiate change, invent, direct, and send — if there are the right incentives for the right people at the right time. Knowledge workers tend to think more of money incentives. Talented people know that money is a by-product of value-added contribution. If you want to transform knowledge workers into Talents, give them the right incentives. Knowledge workers may need a mentor — a person who helps them bridge the gap. Beyond money, Talents are motivated by visions, dreams, missions, and innovations. Talents want to bring something exciting and revolutionary into being. They want to make known the unknown. That is a Talent's creed — to create something that makes a mark.

People Quality Management (PQM)

You can manage only people, not things. You can only lead people — lead them to self-discovery. Leading people takes time. If you don't have the time or the patience to lead, you cannot be an effective leader of anybody, much less of temperamental Talents.

Are you enthusiastic about your role as a leader? Do you exude your enthusiasm for others to catch? Are you always asking yourself how to create the world's most productive and creative work environment? Do you spend the majority of your time with the Talents and other people within your organization? Do you manage by wandering around? Or do you spend the majority of your time in meetings or with your boss or other members of higher management? Is your priority to make your boss happy or to make your people happy?

The answers to questions like these are important to managing people in general, and they are important beyond belief to leading Talent. The boss's primary job is to help his or her people get their job done. All other jobs pale compared to number one: help people do their jobs and create an environment that truly fosters joy of work. I sometimes think of my work environment as a grownup's playpen filled with the tools — oops — *toys* of work. This approach to management is super critical to the challenge of managing Talents. Talents do not respond well to command and control management styles. Talents need freedom and flexibility to work in the ways that are most effective, most creative, and most comfortable for them.

Other vital management approaches include:

- **Practice and foster a winning attitude.** Foster the confidence that you and your team can be the best in the world.

- **Allow participative decision making.** Lead the people most knowledgeable about the subject and responsible for carrying out the decision to make the decision. If you have to make the decision, it is a failure of the process.

- **Use fact-based decision making.** Do this for you, not for the Talents. Talents sometimes pursue feelings, not facts.

- **Use no-fault insurance.** Ask what, not who.

- **Praise in public, pan in private.** Never, never, never embarrass or humiliate Talents. They always leave the corporation, and they will never work there again.

- **Use total honesty, no matter what.**

- **Grant trust.** Don't make people, especially Talents, earn trust.

- **Exude respect to everybody.**

- **Practice and foster the four Cs.** Grow through communication, then cooperation, then collaboration, and finally commitment.

- **Focus on process, not results.** Process measures are leading indicators; results measures are trailing indicators too late to help.

- **Foster mistakes.** Mistakes will be made in any project. Foster rapid mistake making to get mistakes out of the way early. Don't let them turn into problems downstream, where they can only be patched, not fixed, at great expense. This is an unusual but effective approach to prevention.

- **Foster creativity.** Don't get in the way. Be inquisitive, not inquisitional.

- **Be a friend, not a boss.**

- **Ask Talents what they want and need from you, then deliver with great haste.**

- **Stay available.** Don't let time be stolen by bosses and meetings.

- **Treat Talents as customers because they are.** They can go anywhere, and they will if they don't buy what you are selling for a company to work for.

Many other specifics could be listed, but the main idea, not the details, is all that is needed. Be certain that you understand and practice the main idea if you want to attract and keep top Talent.

If all of this seems too difficult, find another line of work. Talent management requires all of this and more. If you can't practice the spirit of Talent management, don't harm the company by staying in a position involving the management of Talent. Change jobs for your sake and the sake of others.

Managers of Talent must address the following questions. How do you get the upside of Talent without the downside? How do you get the best out of Talent? People quality management (PQM) is a way of leading and managing Talent that brings out only the best of Talent and prevents the worst of Talent from coming out. Managing people effectively is the only way to get the organization to perform to its potential and deliver winning products and services. You don't manage quality; rather, you manage the people who produce quality. PQM is all about Talent management. It is the foundation of the *Talent Management System,* which is discussed in chapter 5.

For example, the Six Sigma quality initiative is more than a quality tool — it is a way of inspiring people. Quality products and services are important, but people quality is the most important variable in achieving success. Without proper PQM implementation, an organization is unlikely to achieve good product or service quality. Organizational health mostly depends on the "quality" health of its people. Poor product and service quality damages the company's reputation, but poor people quality can ruin a company.

Most organizations generate a lot of effort thinking about product and profit improvement, but they rarely think about the people side of quality. Transforming total quality management to people quality management is a major challenge for corporations in the twenty-first century.

People quality affects product and profit quality. Management spends a lot of money on fixing problems in product quality to eliminate defects. But often management doesn't want to spend money to prevent problems from arising in the first place. Those talented people who think about the future and prevent quality problems are rarely recognized and rewarded. Without quality people, organizations can't improve product or service quality. For example, alleged defects in some Firestone tires have been suspected of contributing to about two hundred traffic deaths. Firestone management must place more emphasis on product quality as well as people quality management.

Many dot-com companies like Value America and Priceline .com fell due to bad management. Many founders of dot-com companies didn't focus on long-term survival and success. They focused on the short-term concern of how to make a lot of money quickly by going public. They focused on the IPO, not on quality, and certainly not on people quality management.

PQM emphasizes long-term thinking and prevention by recognizing and rewarding people who practice preventative measures. It is designed to create accountability for every job and to supply feedback, assessment, and guidance about job performance.

The Power of Mind: Positive Thinking

Positive thinking increases determination and fosters a never-give-up attitude. With positive thinking, people can overcome major obstacles. Change produces new thinking. Be happy, don't worry. When I get up in the morning, I start the day by asking myself what I can do that day to make something better, to make my corporation better, to improve the quality of life of someone, to do my part to make the world a better place to live.

Create a winning attitude in yourself for today. Positive thinking fosters confidence and determination to win. Adopt a never-give-up attitude. With positive thinking, people can transform stumbling blocks into stepping-stones and create new ways of thinking. When things go wrong, pull yourself out of the funk and push forward on the positive things you can do today. And be sure that you are providing the working environment that fosters the same kind of mental satisfaction that you are seeking for yourself. Get your act together first. Then you can help others.

Mind nutrition requires ten elements:

1. social, political, economic, and financial freedom

2. freedom from worry and fear

3. an environment where people have freedom to take risk, accept new things, and make mistakes

4. freedom of speech

5. infrastructure, especially Internet access

6. a proper training or learning environment and research facilities

7.   internal reward and recognition systems

8.   exposure to great people and talented coworkers

9.   healthy competition

10.   an environment that breaks race, color, and age barriers

The mind needs political, social, and economic freedom. The mind needs a proper environment to prosper. Many Talents can't succeed because they lack political, social, and economic freedom. If people face many political obstacles in their countries, they become frustrated and don't want to do business there. Social freedom is also necessary. Many people in developing countries are illiterate, superstitious, and ignorant. They are less likely to accept change or new things. So it is very difficult to start a new venture there. Economic freedom is one of the most critical factors for success. Where most people live below the poverty line and have to think every moment about earning their daily bread, it is very difficult for minds to germinate.

Talents thrive in a free speech environment. Freedom of speech means that if I report to you, I can just walk in and say, "Yesterday you told me to do this, but I have another idea." Few people dare do that where they work.

Talents thrive in an environment where they are free to act on the most important things without checking with the boss. They need to be free from the mental stress of fear about what the boss will do if they make a bad mistake. Stress and fear distort thinking, stifle creativity, and generally cloud otherwise clear thinking.

Cultivating the mind can create endless wealth for the organization and society. The United States still leads the world in attracting and developing Talent because of its resources and its culture of cultivating minds and sharing knowledge. But cultivating Talent is not limited to the United States.

In India, MIT and the Indian government are working together to launch a media lab. Why is MIT interested in helping India to put together a media lab? Because MIT knows that in India there are many talented people who will work for less money. India as a country will manage the media lab effectively. It will likely be a huge success and will give Indian Talents an opportunity to show what they can do. The poverty of any land can be cured by cultivating minds. The success of any organization or nation depends not only on collecting great minds but also on providing the great minds with a learning environment.

Talent can eradicate poverty from the land. Thanks largely to the software revolution in India, India's gross domestic product is predicted to grow at least 6 percent per year, which is nearly double the average annual growth of the European Union and far ahead of that of many other Asian nations. Indeed, India's software industry earned $5.7 billion in 2000, dramatically up from $50 million in 1991. Market capitalization, $4 billion in March 1999, rose to $104 billion in March 2000. With market fluctuations, it has dropped to around $65 billion. "But from $4 billion to $65 billion is not a fluke," says Dewang Mehta, former president of the National Association of Software and Service Companies, an industry lobbying group that represents seven hundred Indian companies.

Unfortunately, government bureaucracy is stopping India from making even faster economic development. If people want to start a business in Calcutta, it may take them six months. If the same people want to start the same business in Hong Kong it will take them only one day. According to the United Nations' World Investment Report, Hong Kong ranked as the second-largest source of outward foreign direct investment in Asia in 1999.

What's stopping your organization from even faster economic development? Is the bureaucracy to blame? Are new ideas shunned? Is starting something new too difficult? Corporations are like small countries. Talents migrate from oppressive social and political environments. Your Talents will likewise migrate from oppressive environments to environments that have freedom of expression and action without fear of retaliation and that have real opportunity to prosper mentally and economically.

4 The Elements of a Talent-Friendly Organization

Talents thrive in organizations that help them consistently deliver offerings that customers purchase in preference to competitive offerings while returning exceptional value to owners and other shareholders.

Vision is what the company wants to be at a given date in the future. What business does it want to be in? How big does it want to be? How does it want to behave politically and socially? What contribution to society does it wish to make? What culture does it hope to cultivate?

Mission is the purpose of the company — how it intends to achieve its vision.

Strategic intent is the actions and behaviors needed to achieve the vision.

Priorities are set and adjusted periodically to keep the company on course, moving toward the vision. Priorities, for example, might include customer delight and loyalty, employee delight and loyalty, market share leadership, social and environmental responsibility, outstanding community citizenship, sizzling revenue and profit growth, and astonishing return on assets.

Financial priorities are measures of how well people do their jobs and the outcomes of other priorities. Tactical, short-term actions to cut costs and increase sales tend to slow rather than accelerate long-term improvement and growth toward the company's vision and strategic intent. They are deviations, backward steps from the strategic intent — often made necessary by wrong forecasts or wrong actions to adjust to the forecasts.

All priorities should be measurable and quantified. Some priorities differ from the financial priorities in that they are actionable in strategic objectives and tactical adjustments. A company wins by having the best Talent pursuing noble objectives focused on winning at the corporate level, not at the departmental or personal level. The challenge is simply to do whatever is necessary to deliver the best products and services to customers.

Priorities should be worded with a style. Boring priorities elicit boring responses. Strive to put life into the language of business. Bring to mind excitement, commitment, and an attitude of winning. One corporation changed its job titles from words such as "vice president, distribution" to more whimsical titles such as "vice president in charge of getting stuff to customers."

Lighten up, have fun, be creative, foster innovation in everything you do.

With the vision, mission, strategic intent, and priorities in place, the management team can establish a system capable of helping the team achieve the current year's priorities.

Treat Your Best Talents Like You Treat Your Best Customers

As a member of a management team, you want your Talents to buy what you are offering. As with customers of your products and services, if your offerings don't meet the wants and needs of your Talents, they will seek alternatives. And like customers, after Talents have left you, they seldom return.

Behave Like a Supplier

As a member of a management team, you want to offer what your talented people want and need. You want to perform like world-class suppliers of the world's best place to work. Treating all employees like customers has many positive effects. Developing a customer-oriented approach to employees causes the management team members to reevaluate their own values, attitudes, and behavior. Striving to meet the challenge of attracting and keeping Talents sends a clear message that the organization cares about all its employees.

Regarding bosses as suppliers and talented employees as customers runs counter to traditional management models, but in the economy of intellectual assets, Talents carry a brand under which they offer their services. Management exchanges monies and benefits for their services. So, Talents are suppliers of potential intellectual assets and also customers. In exchange for committing their working lives to an enterprise, they expect a fair return, usually in the form of meaning and compensation. Role interchanges between customers and suppliers are common. Both parties exchange goods they possessed for goods they need.

Develop Imaginative Understanding of the Customer Requirements of Talents

Tools and methods for developing customer requirements are well known within marketing departments. So, seek their help in developing strategies for meeting the wants and needs of customer Talents.

Effective methods for assessing the wants and needs of Talents include surveys, interviews, and focus groups. Substantial preparation and planning are required to conduct these activities. It is best to conduct all three because different information is derived from each. A good sequence is:

- focus groups
- interviews
- focus groups
- interviews
- survey

Focus groups and interviews should contain a mix of people who have and have not participated in interviews and focus groups. The questions and the style of interactions are revised after each cycle to reflect knowledge gained from the previous cycles. The survey should go to the entire employee population. Don't forget the managers. They are also employees.

To ameliorate employee fears, use an outside agency. Experienced professionals should conduct the interviews and focus groups and provide feedback to the management team without attribution to individuals. Take special precautions to ensure that employees are confident that their input can't be traced to them.

The survey questions also need to be prepared by talented professionals. Survey questions cannot be ambiguous because there is no face-to-face interchange. In addition, surveys are primarily useful for statistical validations of information derived through face-to-face dialog with customers. Only professionals in the business of crafting surveys know the details of avoiding the pitfalls and getting representative responses.

Finally, don't let the process degenerate into a survey about how happy or unhappy employees are. What you seek are the characteristics of an organization that outstanding Talents want to join for life.

What Do Talents Want and Need from Your Organization?

If you already know the answer to this question, then your organization must be brimming with Talents. If you enjoy a market leadership position, you have a strong foundation from which you can build faster than your competitors. If, however, you are having difficulty attracting and keeping Talents, perhaps it is useful to review the wants and needs expressed by Talents from other organizations.

People factors dominate. Talents consistently cite three needs above all others. The first is *coworkers* with whom they can develop a mutual respect and trust, learn from, bang around ideas with, and collaborate with; and *bosses* with whom they can develop a mutual respect and trust, learn from, bang around ideas with, and collaborate with.

The second most-cited need is *freedom from micromanagement.* Few people enjoy being overly managed. Talents will not tolerate micromanagement: bosses constantly looking over their shoulder and providing unsolicited "how to" advice. Talents want and need — and often demand — freedom to work, freedom to make mistakes, freedom to learn, freedom to innovate, and freedom to pursue the joy of work.

A third need is *freedom from fear.* Talents shy away from organizations that exhibit even tiny amounts of fear. Fear is a strong negative attribute, and it instantly repels Talent.

Other needs include freedom to pursue ideas and passions; a strong culture of values like honesty, trust, respect, fairness, love, kindness, and compassion; freedom to participate in outside activities such as professional societies or universities to stay current and continue to learn; pay for performance; competitive compensation and in some cases opportunities for large awards for large contributions; and a dynamic, changing organization with a winning attitude.

Talent Satisfaction Measurement System

You need to measure Talent satisfaction with your management system just as you would measure customer satisfaction with your products and services. If you call your external system the "Customer Satisfaction Measurement System" (CSMS), then a good name for your internal system might be the "Talent Satisfaction Measurement System" (TSMS). You can measure the effectiveness of these systems by creating a very simple survey for your employees. Following is a template for a TSMS survey. Of course, you can modify this template to suit your needs. The employee should respond to each category on the right.

	Coworkers	Boss	Company
Are real Talents			
Always ready to help			
Enthusiastic teachers			
Intense, continuous learners			
Intense listeners for understanding			
Supportive			
Innovative			
Kind and compassionate			
Honest			
Earnest			
Trustworthy, dependable			

	Coworkers	**Boss**	**Company**
Respectful			
Care about society-environment			
Care about our company			
Care about our customers			
Care about their coworkers			
Care about their boss			
Care about peers-subordinates			
Care about their family			
Exude enthusiasm			
Exude a winning attitude			
Exude a passion for excellence			
Foster rapid change			
Listen more than talk			
Reliably get things done			
Have outstanding interpersonal skills			

Other statements such as "I believe the talent track is fair," "I believe the talent track is beneficial to the company," and "I am satisfied with my compensation" could be detailed. By compiling the data generated from this survey, you can gain a very good sense of employee impressions of the company. Some of these impressions may surprise you.

I invite you to structure a prototype for your own TSMS.

But there is little point to a measurement system unless there is also a system to respond to and act on weaknesses, shortfalls, and problems. For external customers, a response system might be called the "Customer Action Response System" (CARS). For internal Talent customers, a system might be called the "Talent Action Response System" (TARS). Such response systems are typically designed to take immediate action as problems and complaints are submitted.

An employee suggestion box could double as a suggestion box for Talent customers. An employee response council (ERC) could be formed to respond to the inputs. The ERC — call it the "Make Employees Happy Council" (MEHC) — would prioritize the inputs and assign selected items to project leaders, who would be responsible for developing corrective actions. Project leaders might handle simple problems or define projects and form project teams to find possible solutions to more complex problems. Solution proposals would be submitted back to the MEHC for review, revision, and implementation. The council would be composed of representatives from line management, individual contributors, and the human resources department. An annual or biannual TSMS survey could track progress in making major corrections.

If you believe that you don't have time to implement and manage such a system, you're wrong. In the Talent Era, managing people must be the number one priority. Otherwise, there is little chance of attracting and keeping Talent, and without an adequate base of Talent, there is no chance of winning the competitive race.

Organizational Management System

A winning organizational management system (OMS) has nine elements that are central to attracting and retaining Talent, and each element has known best practices. It is important for you to walk through and understand the following list. Afterward, we will discuss the new terms and some that were discussed earlier.

Customer focus system for Talent

- Imaginative understanding of customer requirements
- Customer engagement process

- Customer requirements translated into company measures
- Customer Satisfaction Measurement System
- Customer Action Response System

Performance and satisfaction measurement system

- Talent Satisfaction Measurement System
- Talent Action Response System
- Make Employees Happy Council
- Talent Management System

Participative management system

- Management by wandering around
- Management by participation
- Management by process
- Management by projects
- Responsibility, authority, accountability definition process
- Participative decision making
- Open door practice

Change management system

- Continuous change process
- Rapid deployment process
- Benchmarking

Constant innovation system

- Innovation institute
- Benchmarking
- Six Sigma and Design for Six Sigma
- New product development process
- Training
- Idea seeding and cultivation funds
- Champion process

- Sponsor process
- Project assessment process
- Intellectual asset management process

Project team formation process

- Cross-functional team formation and building process
- Team building process
- Camp meetings

Employee development system

- XYZ management
- Performance assessment and enhancement processes
- Career planning process
- Four Cs process (communication, cooperation, collaboration, commitment)
- Talent scorecard

Human resource management system

- Training
- Recruiting
- Rapid deployment process
- Talent tracking process
- Management of performance assessment and enhancement process
- Management of career planning process
- Benchmarking
- Placement
- Personnel issues resolution
- Two-tier compensation system
- Reward and recognition process

Financial support system

- Talent track fund
- Idea funds
- Financial projections
- Activity-based costing (ABC accounting process)

Although this is a long list, it includes only those items that are central to attracting and retaining Talent. Common human resource (HR) practices not directly involved in supporting activities to attract, keep, manage, and identify Talent are not listed.

The less familiar or more important elements of the preceding organizational management systems are briefly described next.

Customer Focus System for Talent
There are five best practices of a customer focus system:

Imaginative Understanding of Customer Requirements
Strategies, tools, and methods for understanding customers' wants and needs should be utilized.

Customer Engagement Process
Handing customer requirements over the wall from marketing to a development team guarantees a shallow understanding rather than a deep imaginative understanding of what customers want and need. Strategies, methods, and tools for getting everyone involved in meaningful face-to-face interactions with customers should be taught and utilized.

Translating Customer Requirements into Company Measures
Any organization that develops goods or services for customer use should utilize quality function deployment (QFD) to understand the voice of the customer and translate it into the voice of the company.

Utilizing the Customer Satisfaction Measurement System (CSMS)   CSMS data provide a rich listening post for gathering customer information.

Utilizing the Customer Action Response System (CARS) CARS provides another rich listening post.

Performance and Satisfaction Measurement System

This system has four elements: the Talent Satisfaction Measurement System, the Talent Action Response System, the Make Employees Happy Council, and the Talent Management System. The TSMS provides most of the data that were intended to be gathered by the 360-degree performance appraisal system using a context that should be more acceptable to managers. The company can decide in the context of its own culture to what degree normal and Talent track employees who respond to the surveys should be kept anonymous. Most Talents prefer an open system in order to get more detailed feedback. Employees working for participate-and-support-style managers (a strong sign of management talent) are anxious for interactions, have no reason to fear, and are, therefore, willing to sign their names. Employees working for command-and-control-style managers are seldom willing to sign their names or participate in a face-to-face feedback session for fear of reprisal. Such managers are strong, instant-acting poison for Talent.

Participative Management System

There are seven elements in this system:

Management by Wandering Around   Get out and about. Go to peoples' offices and workplaces. Initiate casual conversations. Ask questions. Listen intently. Be a friend, not a boss.

Management by Participation   Participate as if you were a peer. Get involved. Solicit help with your issues. Involve others in making decisions that impact them.

Management by Process   Foster a passion for excellence in executing a process. Don't obliterate the process by demanding results now. Good execution of good processes consistently yields good results. Shortcuts dramatically increase the risk of bad surprises. Foster quality of events in the process, not quick results. Process events are leading indicators. Results are lagging indicators of problems found too late.

Management by Projects   Projects are the means to get things done. Lists of action items do not cause action. Projects do. Projects call for people to be assigned, resources committed, schedules made, objectives and goals established, and an ongoing assessment process to track progress and fix process problems. Projects have a beginning, a middle, and an end with commitments to do the work. If you want something done, don't e-mail an action item. Instead, go to a potential team leader's office and discuss what would be required to do a project to accomplish your objective. Then it will get done.

Responsibility, Authority, Accountability Definition Process
Responsibility always exceeds authority, and that is okay. It is not okay for people not to understand that they are expected to take responsibility to get things done even if the actions exceed their authority. However, all persons in the organization need to understand what they are responsible for, what their authority to act is, and what they are accountable for. Then they know the rules and when they are breaking them to get things done.

Participative Decision Making   Involve those who know most about the topic at hand and those who will have to carry out your decision. When possible behave as a facilitator. Let the knowledgeable people make the decisions that they must carry out. If you have to make the decision, regard it as a failure in your facilitation skills.

When the team makes the decision, the members understand what it means and how to carry it out. And they are committed to their decision.

Open Door Practice   Schedule time when anyone can drop in and chat unannounced. Schedule different times for scheduled drop-ins.

Change Management System

There are three elements of this system:

Continuous Change Process   The key to successful change is practice. To get good at anything requires practice. Changing a corporation is no different — it requires practice.

Rapid Deployment Process   The comments in reference to "practice makes perfect" in implementing change apply to deployment processes. In the GE *2000 Annual Report,* Jack Welch stated that GE could deploy new practices created in headquarters to full implementation throughout the company within one month. Clearly, some new initiatives such as GE's exceedingly successful deployment of Six Sigma and, more recently, Design for Six Sigma, take years, not months. Nevertheless, GE's deployment capability contributes strongly to its industry-leading successes attributed to Six Sigma and Design for Six Sigma.

Benchmarking   Benchmarking is a key methodology in every aspect of the business. It is the engine of change. Change without benchmarking is a fool's mission. To do so is more expensive, takes longer, has higher risks, and produces less-effective outcomes than spending the upfront time and resources to find best practices for your continuous change process.

Constant Innovation System
There are ten elements of this system:

Innovation Institute   An innovation institute is a powerful change agent. The function of an innovation institute is to constantly search for best practices in the broad arena of innovation, select the best practices that are promising, internalize them into the innovation institute, adapt or tailor them for application within your company, develop training materials, train the trainers, and train and deploy the new best practices throughout the company, including key suppliers of the traditional sort and Talents as suppliers of the new sort. Successful innovation institutes, sometimes called "design institutes" in manufacturing corporations, are staffed with the best and the brightest full-time Talents and non-Talents. The typical duration within an institute is two or three years. Some choose to make service in an institute a lifetime career. Institutes are best structured with a full-time Talent reporting to very high levels, either the CEO or COO. The successful examples are organized like small corporations with boards of directors consisting of a who's who list of members.

Benchmarking   Benchmarking is one of the primary functions of the innovation institute. It is identified separately because of its key role in searching for the best practices on the planet.

Six Sigma and Design for Six Sigma   Six Sigma and Design for Six Sigma are critical initiatives for every company in the new economy. The focus on innovation tends to detract from taking care of the details to achieve quality and reliability — the greatest weakness of Western manufacturing corporations. Japan continues to deliver products with much high quality and reliability at lower cost than Western manufacturers. And it continues to gain market share in nearly every sector. The trend is forty years old. How much worse does it have to get before we do something about it? Very few enterprises have succeeded in achieving quality and reliability anywhere comparable to those of the best Japanese companies, and they pay the horrendous price of more losses in market share, more lost customers.

The Talent Era tends to emphasize innovation. Innovation needs to be balanced between the pursuit of superior quality and reliability and the pursuit of innovative goods and services. Delivering innovative goods and services more rapidly than the toughest competitors is critical. But it is only part of the game. The other critical part is to deliver high quality and reliability at low cost. The latter is often assigned to the business of Six Sigma. However, breakthrough quality and reliability require intense application of Design for Six Sigma founded on Japanese quality guru Dr. Genichi Taguchi's formulation of *robust design*. A knockoff design process using the words *robust design* does not provide competitive levels of quality and reliability. Six Sigma and Design for Six Sigma combine to raise the bar to new levels of quality and reliability and innovative products and services.

New Product Development Process   This is your process augmented with Design for Six Sigma.

Training   Provide training in creativity and innovation and targeted training in all elements of the constant innovation system, including the function and utilization of the innovation institute.

Idea Seeding and Cultivation Funds   The purpose of an idea seeding fund is to foster innovation within operations. Research centers are chartered to create ideas. The operations idea generation fund is a pot of money committed to support unplanned activities to develop new ideas to some level of feasibility. The idea cultivation fund is intended to carry promising ideas to demonstrable feasibility ready to transfer into engineering as a new design concept or new technology.

Champion Process   Champions are always pushing new ideas vertically up the corporate hierarchy where few, if any managers, have any interest or understanding about the topic that is being championed. Championing new initiatives is career threatening. It is corporate America's version of prospecting for gold in lands protected by the federal government's Environmental Protection Agency (EPA). Corporations have built-in protection agencies that resist exploration of new arenas. They are immune to the disease of new ideas such as the grunt work of improving quality and reliability. Observers of champions suggest that during the early steps of climbing the corporate ladder, ten adversaries are created for every advocate. The adversaries create high levels of noise that send mixed signals to management. In the face of many adversaries, a single champion supported by a small band of advocates, usually the creative misfits, stands little chance of convincing an uncertain manager that the proposed initiative could make big differences.

Sponsor Process   If a champion can find a high-level manager with the wisdom and courage to sponsor and help the champion with the treacherous climb up the organizational hierarchy, the champion has a better, albeit still small, chance of success.

Project Assessment Process   Stand-alone management reviews are a clear manifestation of micromanagement dreaded by team members. They are often punitive in nature and demotivate everyone, including the managers who believe that they helped save the project by their insightful questions and probes. Punitive behaviors repel Talents; supportive behaviors attract them.

A better project review process is self-assessment, peer review, and management review. The output of the self-assessment is the input for the peer review. The output of the peer review is the input for the management review. The process takes no additional effort because the information generated by conducting the steps provides the information needed for a reasonable management review.

Intellectual Asset Management Process   Be sure you have such a process and use it. Inform everyone about its existence and how to use it. Are lab books up to date? Are patents being filed? Are trade secrets being filed? Does everyone know what is proprietary and what is not? Are the people who create intellectual assets being properly recognized, rewarded, and compensated?

Project Team Formation Process
There are three elements of this process:

Cross-Functional Team Formation   Staff the full-time core team on time. Avoid part-timers. Part-timers cannot develop a passion for the program. Which program are they committed to? The financial rationalization of efficiencies is false. Part-timers lose more time in shutdown and startup time than they gain by juggling multiple projects, no one of which can be a passion. If one becomes a passion, the others suffer neglect. Subject matter experts can serve as internal or external consultants on a part-time basis. Late staffing and part-timers cause more program schedule slips and end-of-process firefighting than any other factors. Staffing is the job of senior management with the authority to pull people off their current projects to staff new projects.

Team-Building Process   Have expert facilitators guide intense forming, storming, norming, and performing process.

Camp Meetings   Here the chief joins other members of the tribe as an equal. Camp meetings are intended to foster candid and open dialog among equals without fear of reprisal.

Employee Development System

Along with the Talent scorecard, there are four elements of this system:

XYZ Management   This is part of the Talent Management System, which is defined in chapter 5.

Performance Assessment and Enhancement Processes
Standard performance appraisals, no matter what they are called, are all too often demotivating critiques by bosses. A performance assessment and enhancement process (PAEP) focuses on reinforcing areas of strong performance and capability, developing improvement actions in areas of weakness, and establishing career directions commensurate with an individual's strengths. The objective is to help Talents and non-Talents build on their strengths and contain their weaknesses. Like the project review process, the first step is a self-assessment. The second step is a review of the CSMS data to establish the boss's performance as a supplier to the Talent customer. This step levels the playing field for the game of evaluations. The third step is the boss's assessment in the context of the Talent's self-assessment. The fourth step is codeveloping a plan of actions and projects to enhance the Talent's capability and performance. Over time, some people build their weaknesses into moderate to strong strengths while leveraging their strengths to the benefit of the company and to themselves.

Career Planning Process   This is intended as a collaborative dialog between the boss and the Talent to establish career options that mutually benefit the company and the Talent or non-Talent. It complements the PAEP process.

Four Cs (Communication, Cooperation, Collaboration, Commitment)   There is a saying in Japan that describes how people develop relationships: "First, face to face, then mind to mind, and finally, heart to heart." The process is said to take about ten years between close friends. The four Cs process is an analogous progression of how people work together. The four Cs process might take ten weeks rather than ten years. Collaboration and commitment to team members and the project are the strongest of all performance enhancers. Collaboration spawns powerful passions: a passion for innovation, a passion for excellence, and a passion for winning.

Human Resource Management System

The human resource management system includes:

Training   States of collaboration and commitment between the human resource function and line management function are difficult to achieve. Human resource professionals want line managers to support their programs and guidelines. Line managers want the human resource professionals to support their desires and actions without being overly constrained. The balance of power between the two functions is always stressed. Cross-training in the roles, responsibilities, accountabilities, and authorities of the two functions provides a starting platform for moving from contention to collaboration for the good of the enterprise and the Talents and non-Talents.

Recruiting   Recruiting practices need to change drastically toward treating Talents as customers. During the recruiting Talent process, the enterprise is a supplier, not a customer. The enterprise is trying to sell what it has to offer to a Talent, who may be a reluctant customer faced with many attractive choices. Too often, enterprises focus on evaluating the potential of the Talent rather than on convincing the Talent that their offerings are the best on the planet. Talents are attracted to companies that exude a sincere and passionate need for their services. Do the homework to determine that you want Talents prior to inviting them for interviews. Talents have many choices, and they use them wisely. Treat Talents as high-value customers because they are. I know some companies that actually engage in testing even those they regard as potential Talent and wonder why the best of the best do not accept their offers. Real Talent even refuses to take the "silly" test, and the companies still don't get it.

Rapid Deployment Process   As personnel processes change to support the new economy and the Talent, new policies and processes need to be effectively and rapidly deployed within the human resource function and the entire management team through all levels and across all functions. Needed changes are not cosmetic; they are substantive, often requiring changes in behaviors as well as new administering policies, procedures, and guidelines.

Talent Tracking Process   Special procedures should be established to track the progression of Talent over time. If unexpected detours occur, it is important to respond by determining causes and solving problems if necessary. Unfortunately, as people progress from one manager to the next or as managers change above them, their reported performance can vary from super to poor and back to super with every change. These erratic swings are especially pronounced and distressing with Talent. Dr. Deming had it right. A subordinate's evaluation score depends more on the performance of the boss than it does on the performance of the subordinate. The swings are understandable but wrong. When an egocentric Talent reports to another egocentric Talent, the relationship will be made either in heaven or hell. When one is a solid, contributing, modest, smooth, professional non-Talent, and the other is an egocentric, temperamental Talent with zero interpersonal skills, another class of conflicts can arise. The central human resource function needs to track progress of everyone, but especially the more volatile Talents, and recognize major variations in progress as cause for alarm and take action to resolve problems.

Management of Performance Assessment and Enhancement (PAEP) Human resource function needs to track various factors, such as the relationship of compensation to performance, the relationships between Talents, shifts between the Talent and non-Talent tracks, compensation spread between tracks, compensation progression over time, and large variations from one PAEP cycle to the next. The human resource function is also responsible for managing permanent personnel files and resolving issues and so on.

Management of Career Planning Process Every employee should have an individual career path. Career paths should be developed and periodically revised through meaningful face-to-face meetings between the boss and the employee. If the employee has a complaint, he or she should feel free to raise the issue to the HR function for resolution or arbitration without fear of reprisal.

Benchmarking HR, like all other functions, has the responsibility to benchmark its performance and utilization of best practices. It has the additional responsibility to benchmark, or interchange data with similar companies, to ensure that compensation and benefits are competitive. At the risk of repetition, benchmarking is the engine of change. Without benchmark data, all decisions are made in the dark. Don't assume. Find out. Make fact-based decisions. The world is changing rapidly. Keep up to date through frequent benchmarking, say, every year.

Placement Talent placement changes should be carefully orchestrated between the Talent and all managers involved. Chemistry, Talent aspirations, and management expectations must be aligned to keep Talent happy and productive. Non-Talent placement may be driven more by need and traditional factors. The style of placements should be the same for internal and external placements. Talent outside the enterprise can be very helpful or harmful. Strive to maintain good relations with Talents, no matter where they might be.

Personnel Issues Resolution   Response to employees with problems should always receive immediate and priority attention from HR and management. Unattended complaints spread through an organization like a dry timber wildfire.

Two-Tier Compensation System   Compensation for the Talent track needs to be very flexible with very few constraints on the range of pay and bonuses. Talents are often attracted to startups because of the joy of work and the opportunity to make millions. If they are making lots of money, perhaps not millions, they may be more content to remain with a large, stable company to achieve a reasonable balance between family and work. "Pay for contributions" may be a better mantra than "pay for performance." The notions of return on Talent (ROT) and the Talent scorecard provide the means to manage pay for contributions. Means must be established to prevent general escalation of salaries. Conversely, substantially more money needs to be allocated to competitively compensate Talent. Perhaps the XYZ analysis of contributions of Talent versus non-Talent could be used to set a fixed fund for Talent compensation. The pot would be dramatically higher than the non-Talent pot if the XYZ ratios were utilized directly as guidelines. Don't let traditional concerns of equity and disparity dampen efforts to make large differences between Talent and non-Talent pay scales. If 5 to 10 percent of the people — the Talent — contribute 60 to 70 percent of the value, pay them for their value, perhaps even three times what you pay non-Talent. Two-tier compensation systems have been around for years, and they have served many companies well. Many companies identify high-potential (hipo) employees and put them on a hi-po track with higher pay scales. The difference in scales is normally rather small, and that is the central issue. Talents contribute orders of magnitude more than non-Talents and get paid 20 percent more. That is not equitable. If Talents contribute ten times as much, they should receive at least two or three times the pay of those who contribute ten times less.

Reward and Recognition Process   Even though most organizations have the reward and recognition process in place, few practice the process effectively. The timely reward and recognition process inspires Talents.

Financial Support System
There are four elements in this system:

Talent Track Fund   Determine and allocate upfront funds needed to compensate Talents. Talents don't understand freezes that impact their anticipated pay for contributions. Don't get trapped by traditional thinking and practices.

Idea Funds   The two idea funds are to support idea seeding and idea cultivation. Leading corporations allow their Talents to spend up to 10 percent of their time creating ideas and developing them to feasibility levels. The idea funds provide the monies for equipment, materials, lab space, technicians, and in some instances a portion of the Talents' salary while they are prospecting for new ideas. This insightful leadership attracts and keeps Talents.

Financial Projections   Financial projections are key to planning. What level of resources will be available to the organization? The smooth flow of monies to support Talent from year to year is necessary to avoid the familiar ups and downs in available resources depending on this quarter's earning projections.

Activity-Based Costing (ABC) Accounting Process   ABC accounting practices are consistent with the Talent scorecard. The cost of Talent occurs in the present. The return on Talent occurs in the future. It is important to keep resources spent and income derived at a future time associated with the same activity in order to unambiguously predict and calculate return on Talent.

The OMS characterized here is an upgraded version of what is typically regarded as a good management system. The elements of the system were chosen with a focus on attracting and keeping Talent. Although the number of elements may seem formidable, it contains no more elements than typical management systems. It is seldom that they are all written down in one place. As a sanity check, review the list and note any elements that you regard as unnecessary. After carefully reflecting on their purpose, if you still believe that they are unnecessary, delete them. Then add elements that you believe are not covered. Now you have your customized management system.

All that is left is to document the system, gain management approval, develop the training materials, develop a deployment process, and roll it out to the cheers of the workforce.

Alternatively, keep the system that is in place and devise a radically new system for Talent.

Talent As Customer, Talent As Supplier

In this system, the company treats a Talent as a customer to attract him or her. Then the company reverses roles and treats the Talent as a preferred supplier. The company as the customer and the Talent as the supplier of contributions negotiate a contract for specified contributions, in-process checkpoints, progress payments in accordance with performance against checkpoint specifications, and a final balloon payment upon completion of the contracted contribution. This customer-supplier partnership seems to cut through a lot of the complexity of upgrading a management system just to attract and keep Talent. This is win-win for both the Talent and the company. Are there any hidden problems? Let us reexamine the list of elements.

In this supplier-customer partnership model, there is no need for the human resource function to be involved. Management styles don't have to be adjusted to keep Talents busy and happy. Or do they? How happy is our current supplier base with us as a customer? Perhaps we should behave more as partners than procurement expeditors with our suppliers.

A special Talent track does not have to be created and managed. Of course, the Talent track fund is needed, as are funds to seed and cultivate ideas.

At least the formal performance assessment and enhancement process does not have to be implemented. Or does it? PAEP looks a lot like the first step in a supplier upgrade program.

Well, Talents do not need to be subjected to the external customer focus system. Or do they? Top management has been discussing the value of getting our preferred suppliers focused more on our external customers than on us as their customer. Perhaps we should broaden our customer focus system to include all of our preferred suppliers, not just individual Talents.

Continuing the review of the organizational management system, we soon discover that none of the elements falls off the list because of contracting with Talents as preferred suppliers rather than hiring them as employee Talent. Some elements get redirected toward supplier needs rather than internal employee needs. But they all remain in the system in some form.

Perhaps the solution is to offer both alternatives to Talents, whether they are new candidates or long-term employees, contract or employment. Confident entrepreneur Talents may opt for the freedom of a contract with no requirement to spend so many hours of face time in the office. More conservative Talents may opt for employment. Perhaps the choice provides another feature to distinguish us from others struggling to attract and hire Talent.

Compensation

In the Talent Era, compensation has become a key area of concern for all managers and employees. Talents have figured out that they are free agents and so compensation can be a big issue. However, if employers have done their homework well in the areas outlined earlier in this chapter, issues of compensation should become secondary issues to them. Issues of work environment, combined with a good and fair compensation system, should lure and keep good Talent.

Clearly, I am suggesting a number of new ideas with regard to the management of Talent. Some of those ideas reflecting the compensation needs of the employee have been mentioned in the context of managing and retaining employees. Here I would like to list some of the key compensation components that will help companies retain top Talent and, for that matter, the rest of their employees.

Although financial compensation comes in many forms, here I will focus on salary. This is a fundamental source of expense for the organization, and so a prudent salary policy is necessary. How does a company reward Talents while not inflating the salaries of its knowledge workers to the point where their return on investment is no longer appropriate? The best answer is to have two pay scales for each level in the organization. An alternative is to widen pay scales for all levels of employees.

Let's take the case of widened pay scales first because this is a common practice. Companies have long been faced with the proposition that employees will threaten to leave if they do not get more money. The typical solution in an organization is to widen pay scales. The problem with this is that it gives managers more latitude to increase the pay of typical employees (knowledge workers or even low-level workers) while not giving enough room to compensate talented workers appropriately. This solution can be more costly to an organization than the two-tier process discussed later. The reason is that managers will always feel the pressure to raise wages, and the Talents will lead the upward pressure. Companies tend to pay the same for the same level, and so the result is that some companies pay all workers what they pay their Talents. In a downturn, this means that the effects of overpaying your knowledge workers will be felt. Layoffs will ensue. Because the salaries are still too high, the impact will be that after layoffs there are too few people in knowledge worker positions to effectively support the Talents. This is precisely what has happened at Lucent. With all the layoffs, it will be understaffed and will struggle in the future to remain competitive. It will still have the problem of improper salary levels, and so the problem will not go away until Lucent does something about it.

The alternative is a brighter one. That is to offer two salary ranges for each position. The range for knowledge workers would be narrower, reflecting the return on investments (ROI) of those employees. Another level would be determined by the typical ROI of the Talents in that position (their return on Talent, as discussed in chapter 8). Having two salary ranges allows the organization to have greater flexibility while maintaining a level of fairness and order in the HR department. Management will be able to respond to the needs of Talent when necessary without compromising the integrity of the system. All managers and employees would need to be at least somewhat aware of this system so that discrimination issues are not a factor. Employees could then strive to become Talents. Later in this book we look at the factors that affect determining talented individuals, and so we will not do so here, but those factors would set up a class of Talents who would be compensated under this system. Managers would be responsible for the median level of their knowledge workers' salaries. Arguments would need to be made to upper management to secure a position in the upper pay scale, and their return on Talent would then be measured going out into the future to make sure the investment is justified. The organization would buy in to the wages of the Talents so that the line manager is not solely responsible for determining the salary of the Talents. The effect of this structure is to decrease upward pressure on knowledge worker salaries and to increase the likelihood of retaining and having happy Talent.

Another possibility is to have the Talent work under contract. Even if the person was an employee before, you may feel that this is the best strategy. Although this may be the best strategy, especially if there are HR issues that prevent you from treating the Talent as you would like, there may be some downside in that the Talent is not a full-time regular employee and so may not feel as much a part of the organization as do other employees.

In any event, it is important that budgeting be done with the needs of Talent in mind. Losing talented people is not an option. Taking advantage of opportunities to add Talent is also important. Planning with Talent in mind is a necessity and should be a part of any organization's future plans.

Summary

Management systems continue to serve basic human needs. Organizational management systems need to be renewed to reflect new demands of the times. But their basic structure seems secure. Past experiments of revolutionizing management systems have only slightly improved the basic systems. One more time: Management systems address very basic, daily human needs. Good management systems foster desired attitudes and behaviors. Bad application of good systems, or application of just plain bad systems, fosters deep resentment, distrust, and sometimes disruptive behavior.

5 Talent Management System

The Talent Management System (TMS) is an effective tool for creating a symbiotic relationship between Talent and the organization to dramatically accelerate performance improvements. The TMS is a distinct function within the organizational management system devoted exclusively to attracting Talent, keeping Talent, managing Talent, and identifying Talent. It is administered by the management team in cooperation with the human resource function.

TMS elevates Talent to a visible, exalted position to which others aspire. The TMS should be implemented and communicated as a big deal because it promotes distinct tracks for Talents and other employees. The introduction of a TMS system could create commotion, gossip about the insensitivity of management to people's feelings, complaints of discrimination, outright rebellion, and work stoppages. But if introduced carefully, TMS can also cause people to recognize special contributors in meaningful ways.

Special tracks are not new. Most corporations identify high-potential employees (hi-pos) and put them on a hi-po track with a higher pay scale. Engineering organizations identify gifted engineers and put them on a "dual ladder" track that can extend upward through several vice presidential levels. The same for gifted scientists. Why not the same for other Talents?

The Talent Management System should be a powerful magnet to Talents, demonstrating that the corporation cares about Talents and their joy-of-work needs.

Four Elements of the TMS

The Talent Management System is structured into four elements:

1. **Attracting Talent** describes how to become a strong magnet for Talent.

2. **Keeping Talent** describes how to create and maintain daily working environments in which Talents can productively pursue the joy of work and financial benefits from contributions.

3. **Managing Talent** describes how to treat Talents as customers and create opportunities and freedoms for Talents to stretch for their dream, for the things that make big differences for the company and for society.

4. **Identifying Talent** describes three ways to identify visible and hidden Talents: (1) notice and identify the obvious Talents, (2) use a performance-based identification tool, and (3) use a test-based identification tool.

Benefits of the TMS

New management systems that impact human resource practices often frighten management. New "fads" don't always work. Getting a management system wrong can take down a company. Enormous benefits and minimal risk need to be shown.

The Talent Management System can quickly transform an organization from an also-ran or a laggard to a world-class leader. The TMS is designed to minimize risk. It is a small overlay on whatever system is in place. The overlay resides primarily with line management, not human resources. Human resources picks up some new administrative responsibilities, such as introducing and maintaining a new system that promotes inequities between Talents and others. This is not a new challenge. Hi-po and dual ladder tracks are the norm in manufacturing corporations. The suggested Talent track is no different. Special tracks are very manageable when the portion of the population in them is small and clearly distinguished from the general population. By definition, the Talent population will always be small because Talent is defined by a level of contribution compared to the level of contribution of the rest of the population. If the overall level of capability rises, the bar for Talent status also rises.

The benefits winnow down to winning or losing. In long races, the best Talent with the fastest vehicle wins. The vehicle is the corporation. Being fastest means changing faster than the toughest competitors. XYZ analysis indicates that 60 to 70 percent of contributions come from 5 to 10 percent of the employees, the Talents. The TMS will create enormous excitement.

- Management behaviors will immediately change, at least for those you want to keep. The concept of treating Talent like customers completely changes the paradigm about the roles of employees and managers. Envision writing a stage play about telling a manager that she is now the supplier of "joy of work" to temperamental customers called Talents.

- The Talent Management System will be a strong magnet for attracting and keeping Talent.

- Non-Talents will aspire to become Talents. They will seek guidance about how they can improve to be worthy of becoming a candidate for moving to the Talent track, hi-po track, or dual ladder track.

- Hidden Talents will become visible. The silent ones will feel safe in coming forward.

- External Talents will be knocking on your door to get in.

- If you are first or second in creating a significant Talent pool among practitioners and managers, then your organization will develop a reputation of being the absolutely best place in the world to work. Then you can further increase your Talent pool. Of course, the opportunity to leverage early successes to spiral up is accompanied by the opportunity to trail behind and spiral down.

- Talent can go anywhere, and most of them know it. Be the first to make a big splash about your new Talent Management System oriented around treating Talent like the customers that they are. Then advertise: "We know that you have more attractive opportunities than you can investigate. So do we. We need more Talent. We are truly different. Our very livelihood depends on Talent. We are different, we need you, we know we need you, and we will behave in ways that you want us to behave. And that's different."

- Be first. Catch the best Talent.

Attracting Talents

Attracting Talents, transforming hidden Talents into visible Talents, and keeping the work environment attractive to Talents are ongoing tasks. Talents work for the joy of work. They need to be compensated commensurate with their contributions. Compensation is a tangible measure of how the organization values their contribution, not fluff. "Thank you's" and compliments are nice but meaningless measures. Money per se is mostly a maintenance factor, not a motivational factor for Talents. Treat Talents as customers, and you will attract them.

Explaining the liberal pay-for-performance compensation system for Talents will further attract them. In his article "The Job That No CEO Should Delegate" in the March 2001 issue of *Harvard Business Review,* Honeywell chairman and CEO Larry Bossidy says that no CEO should delegate the job of hiring key people. He feels that the interview process in hiring is the most flawed process in American business. He says you can't spend too much time on hiring and developing the best people. Many of the people he developed in that company later left to become CEOs of other companies.

The relentless pursuit of Talent should be a main management strategy. Most companies can't recruit talented people fast enough. This Talent shortage is the biggest obstacle to growth, and overcoming it can mean a huge strategic advantage. But money alone won't do it. Talented people want to be part of an organization they can believe in, one that excites them.

Here are seven ways organizations can attract Talent:

1. Treat Talent as customers

2. Have a Talent Management System

3. Promise future reward and recognition with stock options, other ownership options, and performance-based pay packages

4. Have a flexible work environment and positive culture

5. Provide proper training and research facilities

6. Practice visionary management and leadership

7. Conduct performance reviews and succession planning

The single most important thing organizations can do to become more attractive to Talent is to create a flexible work environment. To attract more Talent, an organization needs to create an environment that attracts the most talented people to create the knowledge base needed in the organization. Rather than have narrow job functions — "This is the only thing I do and nothing else" — people should feel free to walk around. For example, even though they are working in the marketing organization, talented employees may go to product development and say, "Here is an idea." It may be wild, but still the marketing people should have the freedom to talk about it — and product development should consider the idea. For example, suppose you want to develop a car, and somebody in marketing comes up with a phenomenal car design and concept. Nothing wrong with that. That is the kind of flexible work environment that attracts talent.

Example: Herbert's Recruiting Story
When Herbert returned from his recruiting trip to Company XYZ, all he could talk about was how great the people were. He was so excited he practically screamed about how enthusiastic everyone was about the company and their work. He explained how Joe got out some of the presentations he used to explain his new widget to management. Although the widget was highly secret because the company was in a close race with its toughest competitor, Joe granted Herbert the trust that he would keep the secret. Herbert's friends knew that he could never break such a trust. The secret was in good hands. Apparently, Joe also knew that trust granted is trust secured.

Herbert charged on without taking a breath in an attempt to emulate the enthusiasm exuded by the hiring manager, George. He was astonished by George's explanation of his management style. George explained that he sought out the best Talents that he could find, asked them what they wanted to do, and then firmly instructed them to go do it. Herbert explained how George rushed nonstop to explain that *talent* is an important word. Talented people are different from good people or, to use the vernacular, hi-pos. Hi-pos are usually strong contributors to the daily needs of the projects that they are assigned to. Some Talents could not be successfully assigned to pursue a set of sequential activities in a disciplined way to get a body of identified work done by a particular time. Other Talents could perform "routine work" from time to time if they were given the freedom to pursue their dreams part of the time.

Talents are different and need the freedom to pursue their thing. Talents nucleate new ideas, new ways of thinking, and new ways of doing things. Talented people may or may not fit very well into the culture of the organization; some do, and some don't. Some visibly work hard, and some don't. But they are all special and worth their weight in gold. Yes, they require extra attention, extra management time, and often myriad other strange demands. But they make big differences in totally unexpected ways. They are the spirit and real leaders of the organization.

George went on to explain that the company's personnel systems did not support people outside of the norm very well but that top management had the insight and the trust to let managers identify and work with Talents. This informal system caused some problems, to be sure, a few serious problems. Some hi-pos wanted to be identified as Talents or at least get the special privileges, including the higher compensation afforded Talents. After all, the hi-pos felt they contributed more everyday than the so-called Talents contributed in a year or perhaps a lifetime.

Finally, Herbert said, George lowered his voice, slowed the pace of the conversation, and with deliberate care began to explain what Herbert had expected him to explain, namely, the mission of the organization and how someone like Herbert was needed to fill an important role, not just a position. Herbert recalled that George had a folder on his desk that contained all the formal recruiting materials about the mission and vision of the corporation and how his Advanced Development Department fit into the corporation. He showed the organization chart and what organization Herbert would be in. George continued to explain some of the strengths of the company, including the competitive compensation system, the reward and recognition programs, how much more his company spent on benefits than did most other companies, and, in general, why it was a super place to work.

Herbert stopped and yelled, "All of a sudden George lunged at me, took the written mission statement, wadded it up, threw it in the wastebasket, and bellowed, 'That is how much the mission statement is worth. Our mission is in our heart, not on a piece of paper. That is why we are good at what we do. The few Talents have caused all of us to band together like rebels with a cause and do what's right for society, for our customers, for our employees, for our company, and for our stockholders. We can't even write our mission on a sheet of paper. It changes every day in some important way. We are an undisciplined, dynamic, passionate group of people striving to do what is right. People in other organizations point to us, only partially in jest, as the collection of misfits who can't adjust to normal expectations of more orderly and structured organizations. We collectively strive to create an environment of "freedom to act, freedom to fail, and freedom to succeed." Such freedoms engender a high degree of responsibility, a passion to do what is right for the corporation and for society. That is why we are good, and that is why you should join us.'"

George closed with "Have a good day. I need to walk around to find out what the misfits are doing today." Herbert said that he was so excited that he was scared that he might not get an offer. Herbert went on to explain, "All I did was listen and occasionally nod. He did not ask me anything about my background or interest until his last words as I was closing the door. 'Go home, think about what you would like to do and then tell me so that when I hire you I can firmly instruct you to go do it.'" Herbert said he went home and thought all night about his two hours with George. He did not know what he wanted to do. He kept hoping for a burst of creativity, an idea, any idea, before the sun came up.

Herbert had the good fortune of interviewing at an exciting corporation that attracted and retained Talent. George was a Talent who attracted Talent. Talent attracts Talent. A performance-based compensation package is another key to attracting as well as keeping Talent. At the end of the day, you have to create an environment where Talents feel that they will be free financially. If talented people do not feel that they will be well compensated for their contributions, they will seek opportunities elsewhere and find them. Once on board, if Talents feel, "I am not getting enough money relative to my contribution," Talents won't perform, or Talents will walk.

Keeping Talents

Talents are restless and mobile. To keep Talents happy, treat them like customers. Provide ongoing services that continue to make your company an obviously better place to work and contribute to the world than any other company in the world. Customer loyalty is created by ongoing services beyond the initial purchase. Successful organizations do not take the loyalty of talented people for granted. They constantly try to recruit and keep them and have think tanks at every level. Mutual commitment of the employer and employee characterizes a successful organization.

Joe Liemandt, CEO of Trilogy Software, a fast-growing software firm based in Austin, Texas, says: "Trilogy treats its employees like they are all managers, partners, and shareholders." That is why Trilogy is so successful. But Liemandt's biggest worry is keeping his talented people. He knows they can go anywhere. "There's nothing more important than recruiting and growing people. That is my number one job." Barb Karlin, director of great people at Intuit, boldly says: "If you lose great people, you lose success. It's that simple." The organization must foster an atmosphere that makes its Talents want to stay.

Organizations keep talented employees by doing the following:

1. They treat Talents as customers.

2. They compensate Talents as preferred suppliers.

3. They offer the right compensation, including proper reward and recognition.

4. They conduct meaningful performance appraisals.

5. They design jobs to appeal to talented people.

6. They assign the right Talent to the right jobs.

7. They choose the right location to attract and retain the right Talent.

8. They provide proper training, development, and succession planning.

9. They provide a proper research facility.

10. They balance age, race, gender, and color.

11. They create a challenging environment or excitement in jobs.

12. They communicate candidly without fear of reprisal.

13. They provide unassigned time to seed and cultivate ideas.

14. They create social bonds with Talent through adventures, sports, games, contests, parties, and celebrations. For example, a former IBM manager used to take his twenty-four managers on a white-water rafting trip down the Colorado River each summer. He says, "When you're in white water together, and someone falls out of the raft, and you have to think how to get him back in, that creates deep bonding. At night, at a campsite that is far removed from cell phones and other distractions, the group can discuss different business strategies."

We can create a symbiotic relationship between Talent and the organization. Talents can't be owned forever or even purchased temporarily unless you satisfy them properly. There is no guarantee of lifetime employment of this most critical asset. Corporate growth depends on the growth of individual Talents; and Talents grow faster when an organization grows vigorously. When a proper symbiotic relationship is developed between Talents and the organization, Talents give their physical, mental, and even spiritual support to that organization.

To create a symbiotic relationship with Talents, try these seven actions:

1. Recognize and reward Talents properly.

2. Offer profit-sharing plans or stock options that create a sense of ownership.

3. Measure team and individual performances.

4. Evaluate the performances.

5. Develop a performance-based, semivariable compensation package.

6. Define responsibility, authority, and accountability for each project.

7. Eliminate people who are not performing.

The number one reason why most good Talents leave is because they are not recognized and rewarded. They are frustrated, and the primary source of their frustration is the lack of recognition and reward — social, emotional, and financial recognition. They see their boss get ten times more recognition and compensation than they get from their ideas and work. So they get frustrated and say, "Okay, I am leaving." Smart Talent managers ask, "Who came up with this cool idea? I want to recognize this person personally in front of the entire staff." How often does your organization do that? Without the recognition, talented people will leave. Typically the rewards go to the wrong people. If Talents feel undervalued or exploited, they will leave. When people feel exploited, it doesn't matter how much money you give them, they leave.

Talents must learn to accurately assess the value of their contributions. If they always overestimate the value of their contributions, the organization may let them go. True Talents neither overestimate nor underestimate the value of their contributions. If they do, they can cause dissent and may hurt the company more than they help.

For example, when Talent comes up with a powerful idea, but the organization doesn't buy into it, Talent quits. Most talented people will leave if they receive significantly less financial reward for their innovative ideas while some executives make tons of money. Often Talents are told, "We would like to pay you more or promote you, but you don't have managerial skills." So, the Talents leave — and their former managers are then likely to be laid off because they no longer have the Talent needed to achieve desired results.

Some organizations may want to create a dual ladder so that Talents can climb upward without taking on management responsibilities. Job grades and titles for higher-level Talents on the individual contributor ladder for Talents should be considered. Not all Talents want to be managers. But you want to keep all Talents.

True Talents are people who make a significant contribution. There are people who just make noise, saying, "I've done this, and I've done that." True Talents don't make much noise — they let their performance speak for them. Success to them is in the success of the products or processes they create. Still, in their hearts, they are deeply bothered when they don't get the recognition and rewards for their ideas, especially when others who made a minimal contribution receive the rewards. This is a key point for managers to understand. Talents may not say they need to be recognized, but they are like anyone else, but are more likely to feel slighted. Talents will stay with an organization for ten, twenty, or thirty years only if they are having fun. Having fun means they are contributing something that they believe is important and are being recognized and rewarded for their contributions. They work in a speak-your-mind, freedom-to-act, freedom-to-fail, freedom-to-succeed atmosphere, and they can excel at whatever they do. Most Talents will stay or come back to an organization if they are treated well. They may leave to see if the grass is really greener in another place, but if they were recognized well and treated fairly, they might come back. Few organizations make a concerted effort to recruit former Talents. If and when Talents return, they need to be put in a new position or location or given a fresh challenge. Returning employees need to keep having fun. Most organizations have little long-term memory, and so when Talents leave, they are soon forgotten. If talented people come back, they need a new position.

Managing Talents

Managing Talents may seem a hopeless endeavor. Talents seek freedom and support, not managing. Again, think of Talents as customers. You can't manage customers. You can only provide them with the goods and services they want and need. Determine their customer requirements. Ask Talents what they believe is the most important thing they can do for the company. If it is within the boundaries of the strategic direction of the company, ask them what they need from you and then provide those needs instantly. Act quickly. Delays in service indicate that you don't care — not a message you want to send to temperamental customers.

Managing Talent has to be learned. Managers must know how to get the best out of people and how to strategically place them in the right position where they are not dragged down by routine work. Managers must provide the setting in which their Talents can produce maximum knowledge and maximum innovation and have maximum impact. When strategically managed, Talents will generate maximum return. Many companies don't bother to grow their own Talent or have farms or ways to grow Talent because they don't have anything like a Talent Management System. They think managing Talent is the human resource manager's job. Many managers mistake "people who kiss the manager" for Talents — and they may promote the wrong people. Whom you know becomes much more important than what you know or what you do. This is a common mistake. Don't let politics get in the way of making good decisions. The manager may have a hard time making the proper decision.

Often, the employees will know the Talent better than the manager does. There are a couple of easy ways to solve this problem. The simplest way is for the manager to get an unbiased read from the employees on who is doing the best work. If the manager does it regularly enough, the employees will let down their guard, and the communication will be best. Absent that level of communication, the manager may need a more formal way of ascertaining who might be most talented. The manager might need an independent unit led by a chief Talent officer (CTO) who manages the Talent. In addition, the company could establish a "Keep Talent Happy Council" headed by a chief Talent officer, to provide the guidance and training of the management team. If the organization is having a difficult time analyzing, finding, managing, or keeping its most talented people, something along these lines is a good idea.

Treating Talents as preferred suppliers by spectacularly compensating them for their spectacular contributions will also change the behaviors of the managers whom you wish to retain. The demand for Talent places new demands on management. Managers who attract Talent should be on the Talent track. Those who repel Talent should be somewhere else.

More organizations should have CTOs and Talent management councils whose job will be to manage Talent effectively inside and outside the organization. CTOs must hire the best, use the best, and keep the best. They manage Talent effectively by treating Talents as customers; they compensate Talents as preferred suppliers; they choose the right Talent for right job; they allow Talent to focus on creating and applying knowledge; they create an emotional bond by touching the mind and emotions; they embrace a trust culture; they build trust by talking and listening to each other freely; they present positive challenges to their Talents to increase their performance level — and "positive challenges" does not mean criticism or humiliation but rather constructive coaching and encouragement; they provide a continuous learning environment; they focus on performance; they reward Talent immediately; they build a culture where Talents can turn their dreams into reality; and they create a boundaryless organization where information can flow freely.

Talent Allocation and XYZ Analysis

The success of any project depends on the proper allocation of Talent resources. Talent is a scarce as well as costly resource. Proper Talent allocation prevents overlapping activities. At every level, management must keep at least one Talent on each team. Management should identify the critical activities and create a priority network. Management should allocate its Talents to those activities on a priority basis. More or less allocation of Talents in any department can cause major gains or losses. For example, suppose a company has a superior product in quality, but it is not getting proper market share due to a dearth of Talent in sales, marketing, and public relations. Management should arrange for a balanced Talent network in every level.

XYZ analysis is a powerful way for organizations to manage their workforces effectively. Management should divide its workers into three categories — X, Y, and Z. See figure 5-1.

Category X workers represent only about 5 to 10 percent of the workforce, but they typically produce about 60 to 70 percent of the intellectual or knowledge value. Although 5 to 10 percent of the workforce is a small group, these people are the most valuable. This category X workforce needs much more attention and should be carefully managed. Organizations cannot afford to lose category X workers because they are difficult to replace. Category X people are the top Talents of the organization.

Category Y workers represent about 25 to 30 percent of the workforce; these knowledge workers produce about 25 to 30 percent of intellectual or knowledge value.

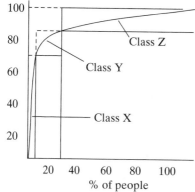

Figure 5-1 XYZ curve

Category Z workers represent 60 to 70 percent of the workforce and produce 5 to 10 percent in total intellect or knowledge value.

XYZ analysis clearly shows which people are the organization's greatest assets. Larry Bossidy, chairman and CEO of Honeywell, said: "At the end of the day, we bet on people, not strategies." But it's a blind bet if managers don't monitor their Talent assets. XYZ analysis clearly identifies the people who are valuable to the organization, and management must pay special attention to keep these people. Management can decrease turnover of category X Talent by doing XYZ analysis.

For example, suppose three people come up with a blockbuster idea that brings in a lot of revenue for the company. If the company doesn't know who those three people are, the company will likely think of each of them as "just another employee" and fail to recognize or reward them. The talented people who come up with great ideas need to get some recognition, perhaps in the form of a promotion or bonus. They are a select breed. Without them, the organization fails to evolve. And yet often instead of being rewarded, such top Talents see others who had little or nothing to do with the creation of the product get all the rewards. So, a frustrated Talent may say, "My boss made five times more money out of my work. Who cares about this company? I am leaving and going to the competition."

To classify workers into X, Y, and Z categories, you have to assess the value of their knowledge contributions. Sort the workforce members according to their value contribution. Constantly monitor the X category, then the Y category. Evaluate how the company can effectively manage those talented people. Create a contingency plan for the event that you lose a significant percentage of people in the X category. Over the years, I've talked with several senior executives of major corporations who confidently told me, "Absolutely. We know who our top Talents are," often referring to the management team. But, are these people the true Talent of the organization? Often they are usually people who kiss up to the boss — who play politics.

When allocating Talent, management should follow six steps:

1. Set the business goal or objectives

2. Develop an action plan or develop each division's goal to meet the business goal

3. Identify the strengths and weaknesses of each division to meet the goal

4. Assign new Talents or train existing Talents to overcome the weaknesses of each division

5. Constantly monitor the performance of each division

6. Take corrective actions if necessary

Soccer is a great analogy of Talent allocation. In a soccer game, it is difficult to win a match by putting all ten players (excluding goalkeeper) in one position — like forward, midfield, or defense. According to the team's strategy, you have to keep some players in each sector to win the game. One team may keep four players on defense, two at midfield, and four in the striker position. Or it may keep four players on defense, three in midfield, and three at striker. A good coach fields a balanced team who has a good defense, a good midfield, and a good striker to win a game. Similarly, managers should keep Talents in each division as needed.

Today business is a team game. It is very difficult to run a business by having an individualistic mentality. If a true Talent team is formed, team performance will be better than individual performance. The team increases the knowledge level of every Talent, and that ultimately increases the performance level. The chances of taking a wrong strategy or making a wrong decision will be less. Also, changing direction or deploying plans is much easier. If everybody is part of the change process and believes in it, a learning climate is created. Talent always wants to learn. If a Talent team is formed, members on the team share their knowledge and learn from each other, which creates a true "learning organization." Talent teams are better than individual Talents because the organization is less dependent on one particular Talent. If for any reason that one Talent left the organization, the organization has others who can pick up the slack.

Identifying Talents

Talent shortage is often the biggest obstacle to a company's growth. More companies need to grow their own Talent, instead of just hiring Talent. Hiring Talent away from a competitor creates a war mentality. In fact, the personnel market is often called the "war for Talent" because companies are hiring (stealing) Talent from their competitors.

Some people cast an unmistakable aura of talent. Others are hidden by impersonal company bureaucracies or overbearing bosses. External people may or may not carry a brand as Talent. Internal or external, put the obvious Talents on the Talent track with significant and immediate compensation appropriate to the Talent track. When uncertain, go prospecting. Prospecting for scarce, valuable resources is an honorable profession. If your apparent gold turns out to be "fool's gold," throw it back and try again. Talent assessment tools are introduced later and in the context of a Talent scorecard to help identify and guide potential Talents.

Year after year, I come across managers who do not know how to identify talented people. Over the years I have met many bright men and women, but management fails to use them effectively. They are frustrated Talents and are therefore unproductive Talents. If management does not use these Talents properly, someone else will. Big benefits come from identifying Talents within the company before hiring new employees.

Identifying your own Talents before hiring new Talents is beneficial because existing Talents already know the strength and weakness of the organization; they are already familiar with the culture; they already know what corrective steps are needed to improve; they take less time in action or implementation of any strategy or idea; and identifying them eliminates recruitment costs. If you still need to hire Talent, and you almost certainly will, visible internal Talent will help attract outside Talent. Talent attracts Talent.

Employees can change behaviors; head-down, obedient doers of what is asked can explode into dynamic leaders of big ideas that can make big differences to your corporation. But they can do this only if they are given freedom to explore and act, the encouragement to champion new ideas, support in championing ideas when the opposition gets tough, bosses who devote the time and energy to listen for understanding and even work on and add to Talent's new ideas, and the experience of being rewarded with a "thank you," rather than chastised, for out-of-the-box ideas. In other words, they need a whole new environment that fosters creativity, not just the daily grind of executing a project. Such environments have transformed wimps into tigers, really strong, agile Talents. The challenge is to find the tigers hiding as wimps. It is certain that there are some such people within your organization. Find them and free them. That is what the Talent Management System is all about.

Conversely, all employees have to be accountable for what they do. If some people don't perform, get rid of them. If you want to move fast, you have to get rid of dead weight. You can't afford people who just go to work from 8 to 5, check e-mail, or surf the Net. This is the flip side of what the Talent Management System is all about.

Talents within the organization often stand out as different. Bosses, peers, and subordinates all recognize obvious Talents. However, some Talents are hidden by the system. Some Talents are quiet, unassuming, mild mannered. Such people are sometimes difficult to identify as Talents. In these instances, other assessment tools can be used.

The first method of identifying Talents is to pay attention, notice, explicitly identify them, and put them on the Talent track. Two other methods are tools: the performance-based identification tool and the test-based identification tool.

Performance-Based Identification Tool

This tool uses a current performance appraisal system coupled with dialog with current and past bosses. Dialogs with peers and subordinates might also be conducted. The collection of existing information becomes an assessment tool when it is used to assess and make judgments about who might be identified as potential Talents. This is a process of assessing past performance and contributions to predict future capabilities within a new set of circumstances. This tool is the method commonly used to identify hi-pos. With changes in criteria against which employees are identified, the same methodology can be effectively applied to identification of Talents. The performance-based identification tool has the advantage of not needing to explicitly involve candidate employees. This feature makes it a useful screening tool to identify promising candidates who might then be asked to participate in the test-based identification tool.

Test-Based Identification Tool

As its name implies, the test-based identification tool intensely involves candidates. Testing should be judiciously used as a complement, not a replacement, to management judgment. Some people just don't do well on tests, especially when the outcomes might be perceived as career threatening. Other candidates test better than they actually perform.

Testing for special positions such as dual ladders is common and generally effective. An important benefit of test-based systems is that they provide all employees the opportunity to apply to take the test. Performance-based systems are utilized by management in top-down processes, making it awkward for people to nominate themselves.

The test-based tool consists of attribute scorecards and a balanced scoring methodology. Like the performance-based identification tool, the test-based identification tool is applicable only to known, internal candidates. An example of a Talent scorecard is shown in figure 5-2.

Talents may have special expertise in certain areas, or the company may need to search for a particular type of expertise. Complementary scorecards can be developed for special purposes. Examples include leader, individual contributor, and subject matter expert scorecards.

The scorecard in figure 5-2 is only an example. The company, and perhaps the organizations within the company, needs to decide what attributes are the most important within its culture. Attribute lists should be generated by a carefully selected group of representatives from multiple levels and multiple functions within the company.

Scorecard Entries   The first column of the scorecard contains a list of "Attributes" that a true Talent would be expected to have. The second column, "Evidence," provides spaces to enter the form of evidence that is used to score the degree to which a person exhibits the corresponding attributes. Two objective measures (observation, fact) and two subjective measures (aura, judgment) are suggested as effective types of evidence. The third and fourth columns provide for entering self-scores and jury scores. The self-scores allow individuals to score each attribute as they assess the degree to which they possess and practice that attribute. Colleagues selected to serve on a "jury of peers" enter the jury scores.

Seven-Step Scoring Process   The scoring process consists of seven steps:

1. Selecting a Jury
The jury is a group of coworkers selected to examine the evidence and vote on the strengths of the evidence for each of the listed attributes (see figure 5-3). The use of a jury is common for this type of task, whether the jury is a group of customers being asked for its requirements, a jury of coworkers examining management styles,

TALENT SCORECARD			
Attributes	**Type of Evidence**	**Self-Scores**	**Jury Scores**
1. Innate skills			
2. Intellectual strength			
3. Inquisitive			
4. Creative, innovative			
5. Passion for work			
6. Works hard			
7. Works smart			
8. Stretch mentality			
9. Continuous learning			
10. Leadership			
11. Passion for excellence			
12. Exudes infectious enthusiasm			
13. Completes projects			
14. Makes fact-based decisions			
15. Dependable			
16. Fosters change			
17. Passion for action			
18. Passion for winning			
19. Recognizes own strengths and weaknesses; soars on strengths and contains weaknesses while striving to improve over time			
20. Listens intently to understand rather than to respond			
21. Confident			
22. Treats mistakes as evidence of action and opportunities to learn			
23. Committed to enterprise			
24. Founded on values and principles — honesty, trust, respect, morals, no gossip			
25. Thinks out of the box or in the box as needed			
26. Balanced styles and orientations — intertwines left and right brain thinking and the four styles: participative, directive, analytical, global as appropriate to a situation			
Totals			

Figure 5-2 Talent scorecard

or a jury of coworkers identifying Talents. To identify a potential Talent with management responsibility, the jury should include a minimum of the boss, a supplier peer, a customer peer, and a subordinate. It is best to have a second representative from the boss's level and a second subordinate, totaling six to eight members. In the spirit of court proceedings, the candidate should select half of the members and the boss the other half.

2. Selecting and Understanding Evidence
The notion of selecting two objective and two subjective types of evidence has been mentioned. One effective scheme is:

Observation: You see it consistently occur.

Aura: Your feelings about the Talent. Aura is *fuzzy* but important.

Judgment: The Talent's behaviors suggest it to be true.

Fact: You strongly believe it to be true. It is verifiable.

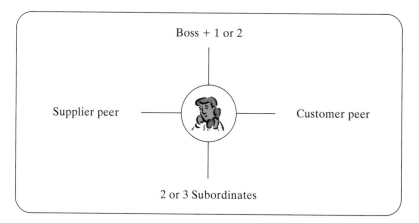

Figure 5-3 **Jury selection**

The scoring process may seem too dependent on opinions and subjective judgments. For any single attribute scored by a single person, the process would be flawed. However, long lists of attributes combined with multiple jury members tend to average a large number of scores toward a mean that is likely to be close to reality. In addition, the more the attributes are stratified, the easier each attribute is to diagnose and score. Finally, the analysis of scores (which will be discussed later) may reveal inconsistencies that the jury members can strive to resolve.

3. Self-Scoring
The Talent should make a self-assessment and score himself or herself. Self-scoring serves several purposes. It helps the Talent understand the process. It involves the Talent in the process. It provides the opportunity to explore any major differences about how the Talent perceives himself or herself and how others perceive the Talent. It provides a consistency check for the analysis activity.

4. Jury Scoring
Any number of scales may be used for scoring, such as the 1-to-5 scale, where 3 is taken as the average for the organization population. A method that focuses attention on comparisons to average rather than numerical evaluations is to use pluses and minuses designated either with p's and m's or +'s and −'s. The highest scores for a single attribute are ++ and −−. Above the average is +, below is −. Assume that the scorecard has twenty-six attributes. The highest possible bottom line score would be twenty-six times ++ or fifty-two counts of +'s. The lowest score would be fifty-two negative counts. An average score would be zero or "s." It is best to enter s's to simplify bookkeeping while doing the scoring. However, s's are not summed because their numerical value is zero, and the sum of zeros is zero. See figure 5-4.

The + +, +, etc. scoring is equivalent to a 1-to-5 scale, except it focuses on comparisons to average rather than numerical values.

| 5 |
| 4 |
| 3 |
| 2 |
| 1 |

| + + |
| + |
| s |
| − |
| − − |

Figure 5-4 **Jury scoring process**

5. Averaging Scores of Jury Members

Averaging is straightforward. Add the scores from all jury members for each attribute and divide by the number of jury members. Enter the averaged score for the attribute.

6. Analyzing the Scores

Analyzing the scores shows the strengths and weaknesses of the Talent as well as the behaviors and feelings of the members of the jury.

1. Look for inconsistencies in the raw scores of the jury members. If one score is dramatically different from the others, strive to understand what the member with that score used as evidence and what is behind the different perception. Resolve if possible and feel free to change scores: either the group of similar scores or the seemingly out-of-step score. If the members cannot resolve the differences, then average and enter the scores.

2. If there are wild variations between all of the scores, again try to resolve. If no one will change his or her scores, then average and enter the scores.

3. If the lack of consistency in scoring persists through many of the attributes, complete the scoring process and consider whether to repeat the total scoring process. Often, a second pass, after discussions about each of the attributes,

leads to much more consistency in the scoring. Compare the total averaged scores of the first and second passes. Very likely, they will be very close in spite of the apparent inconsistencies. If the bottom line scores are different, then take the second pass as the score.

4. Compare the averaged jury score with the self-score line by line for each attribute and the bottom line totals. If major discrepancies emerge, one or all of the jury members should meet with the Talent to present, discuss, and understand the source of the discrepancies. The jury can then decide whether to modify scores.

5. If there is a consistent biasing between the two scores, ignore it for now. It will receive consideration in the next step.

6. Decide whether to include the self-score with the jury score. This is an opportunity for the jury as a whole to influence the scores and the outcome. Take the opportunity with reasonable prudence.

Working through these suggested actions normally improves the confidence in the methodology to reliably discriminate between the potentials of the Talents within the organization to rise to the top (whatever *the top* may mean).

7. Normalizing Scores to a Common Scale

Assume a scale of 1 to 11 and characterize the numerical values as indicated. See figure 5-5. The general formula for normalization of scores to some scale range is:

$$\frac{\text{Score}}{\text{Maximum Count}} \times \text{Scale Range} = \text{Position on Scale}$$

For example, assume a total of twenty-six attributes for a score-card. When all scores are $++$ or $--$, the maximum of fifty-two counts is realized. Assume the bottom line score of forty. Then the score $= 40$, the maximum count $= 52$, and the scale range $= 11$, or: $(40/52) \times 11 = 8.46$.

The test-based Talent identification tool may appear somewhat daunting at first, but with practice it becomes an efficient tool in the manager's tool kit. It will come to be perceived by employees, potential Talents, Talents, managers, and human resources as a mutual benefit to all. Properly administered, it is a tool that fosters socialization between all those involved. It is not a dreaded performance appraisal system. It is more of a career guidance system.

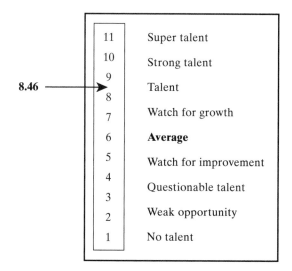

Figure 5-5 Normalizing scores to a common scale

The Challenges of TMS

If you feel that there is a lot of untapped potential in certain people and that you're not getting the full performance out of them, but you don't want to fire them, you might give them a wakeup call to get that talent out of them, to get them to perform better. You might select these people to participate in the test-based identification tool. And you might involve them in adventurous games together so they can develop a social bond.

Most corporations confuse Talents with knowledge workers. Talents may have devised a prevention strategy or a phenomenal innovation, but it may not save or make the company immediate money, and so they are ignored. I know hundreds of engineers who have come up with phenomenal innovations and did not receive any promotion, recognition, or reward — nothing. Because they are talented, they don't want to kiss up to anybody. But if they don't, they are out of the loop. They are not selected to go to a management program. In our society, the big problem for Talent is the internal politics. The more we can break that political barrier, the more Talent can contribute. Talent seeks performance-based, not politics-based, environments. Often senior managers will tell you they have some kind of Talent Management System in place, but they are really talking about their personal preferences or the company political system. True Talents avoid political environments. Typically Talents don't show much interest in politics because of their professional pride. To them political game playing is a waste of time. To them it is not a valid, value-added contribution to the organization. If I am Talent, I need a free environment. Even if I am just an associate, I need to feel that I can discuss anything with the top executive.

By using TMS, managers can properly deploy the skills of talented employees. Many talented people do not produce significant results — due to the lack of a proper TMS. The same talented people working in an organization that uses a TMS will produce better results.

Companies for the most part have some kind of human resources plan, and they certainly have standard procedures to follow. But it is not unusual to find the department to be very bureaucratic. The best companies going forward will have a Talent Management System that operates as a separate or semiautonomous unit. HR management includes every employee. TMS involves only those deemed to have talent. The TMS unit has the responsibility to keep track of the talented people. Organizations are starting to use TMS as the need for Talent has become much clearer in recent years. In the past when you joined an organization such as GM or Ford, you typically wanted to make a career out of it. For the most part, this is no longer the case. So talented people are becoming tough commodities to find and keep.

Summary

The Talent Management System is for managers, not for human resources. TMS is a strategic, transformational initiative. The notion of Talent as customer can change the behavior of managers in ways that can benefit the entire organization. Even tough command-and-control-style managers might be motivated to lighten up, develop better motivational skills, and balance the use of a stick with the use of a carrot. The existence of TMS will help attract and keep the best and the brightest Talents. It will set your enterprise above in the minds of those inside and outside the organization.

Adopt, adapt, and become adept at the Talent Management System. Adopt the basic construct as presented in this book. Adapt it to fit your organization and become adept at using the system to attract, keep, and inspire the Talents to new levels of achievement. The new standard of performance set by the Talent track will cause all employees to strive for better performance.

6   The Growth Rule

Talents thrive in challenging environments that feature grass-roots education for everyone. The more successful an organization is, the more challenging its culture. "Challenge your colleagues, challenge your subordinates, challenge your boss, and challenge yourself" is becoming the new mantra for success. Challenge does not mean humiliation or criticism. It means support and encouragement. Internal challenge helps people to face the tremendous competitive challenges outside the organization. It is difficult to keep Talent without positive challenges. This chapter describes how to issue positive challenges to stimulate growth and discusses the difference between positive and negative challenges.

Positive Challenge

You can attract Talent and manage Talent, but the question at the end of the day is, "Are your talented people growing, or do they feel that they don't need to grow?" This is a growth rule that applies to people who are not talented as well as to people who are talented. Many people are too fearful to challenge their bosses. Historically, this has not been a winning move. Sometimes bosses may not challenge talented people due to lack of knowledge.

Most managers talk about challenge, but few really practice it. When I talk to middle and senior managers, they talk about creating a challenging environment, but when I talk to them individually and ask, "How many times do you challenge your boss? How many times do you say, 'We aren't doing this right. This is the way it should be'?" I don't find that. An environment of fear will stifle the creativity of the people and will allow bad processes to continue. Talented people respond well to positive challenge. Talent has a "what's next?" mentality. If somebody challenges me, I can learn something from it, and I can do something better.

Positive challenges enhance the performance of Talent. Challenging someone based on knowledge represents a positive challenge. Sometimes bosses criticize their subordinates without having the proper knowledge or data — a negative challenge. When colleagues challenge each other, they learn from each other and share their knowledge. This is a positive challenge.

Positive challenges increase the knowledge of Talents. Knowledge grows faster within the company. Intellectual assets appreciate faster. A continuous learning environment is created, bureaucracy is limited, and trust is built, allowing Talents to share more with each other.

Rather than kiss up to their boss, Talents challenge their boss. Some people always want to please their boss by accepting their boss's strategy and directives without question. They always obey their boss — wrong or right. They think that if they blindly follow their boss, they will be rewarded. If Talents don't believe what their boss says, they do not accept it.

Every corporation faces competition in every aspect of business, and this competition will only increase in the future. To compete with these outside challenges, organizations need to create an internal challenging environment where Talents challenge each other positively and create the right strategy, the right products, and the right services. Positive challenges help a company face challenges from competitive organizations by increasing efficiencies, performance, and knowledge of the people. Positive challenges create better products, strategies, and services. Positive challenges create a sense of urgency to create something better.

To create a challenging environment, organizations must:

- Bury bureaucracy and rigid hierarchy

- Try to attract and keep true Talents

- Create a continuous learning environment

- Reward performance

- Remove color, race, age, and gender barriers

- Create a fearless environment

As a manager without challenge, you may not know that what you believe is right. What happens if you do not know the solution to a specific problem? If you have been constantly challenged, you will know whom to go to for the right answers, the honest answers. Challenges help validate or refute beliefs. You have a team whose ideas and opinions you value. The team will help you solve your problem. But when you face a challenge, you will have to prove your viewpoint based on knowledge and performance. Challenge is also a way of finding Talent or understanding what level of talent you have in the organization. Non-Talents avoid challenge because they fear that if somebody challenges them, and they don't have an answer, they might lose their jobs, or their boss won't be happy. You have probably seen the "I don't know" dance. The challenged person dances all around the question or challenge without responding directly to it in an effort to cover his or her ignorance. You can create an environment that has just the right challenge. Every Talent has to be held accountable for performance by earning a high Talent score, knowing that the organization needs a high return on Talent.

Create an environment with little bureaucracy. Yes, you will still have a boss, but you can open your boss's door or send him or her an e-mail anytime. If you believe you have a better idea than your boss, then your boss should be totally open to it. However, much of the time the boss is not so open to new ideas that challenge his own thinking. He may even withhold rewards for exceptional performance. If people do their jobs much better than expected, they should be rewarded for their performance. When non-Talents see that Talents are bringing challenges to the environment and that they are being rewarded for it, then the non-Talents will either improve or self-select out of the environment.

Grass-Roots Education

Grass-roots education involves training the entire staff, without discrimination. Often, management neglects to provide any training at the lower levels. At one U.S. manufacturing facility, managers were changing the spreadsheet analysis software from Lotus to Excel. Although the managers were trained in using Excel, none of the other employees was trained, even though they would be the main users. Six months later, the trained managers were no longer using the new program and passed it down the line to those employees who had never been trained in the first place. The company spent millions of dollars on this change, but ultimately the proper people did not get the training, and so it didn't work out.

Management can't train all employees equally, but management must provide minimal education to all employees. For example, in a Six Sigma program, managers can't train all the employees as black belt or green belt, but they can provide basic knowledge of Six Sigma to all employees. When all workers have a basic knowledge of any program, they will find it easier to implement that program.

Management must monitor the results of training programs. Corporations spend millions of dollars on training programs, but the positive outcomes of those training programs are often limited. Management should monitor how much it spends on training and how much it gains from that training. Management can monitor the results of training by:

1. Creating a project-based training

2. Applying the training on a project where workers can show the results

3. Implementing the training program to create an immediate benefit and ensure viability

4. Creating a measurement system (metrics) to track the results

5. Selecting the right people to use this training

Train the right people — people who can implement the ideas learned from the training. Create hands-on training. Provide resources to apply the learning. Give employees the freedom to apply the training. Classroom training without mentored, on-the-job application of the content is incomplete. Classroom training is the precursor to developing expertise in the subject. Expertise is developed through practice under the guidance of a mentor. Learning to read music and the location of keys on a piano does not make you even a novice piano player. You learn to play the piano by practicing under the guidance of a piano teacher.

Change is more difficult without grass-roots education of all employees. When management tries to introduce change, people may be fearful or resistant. People fear that change may eliminate their jobs, so there is a tendency to not want to accept the change. But if management can teach every employee why this change is important, management can change anything. Grass-roots education helps to bring about proper implementation.

Whether you must implement a new computer system or company strategy, you need education and training to ensure proper implementation. Some organizations spend millions of dollars training employees in the use of specific tools, and yet these employees do not use these tools in their jobs. That's like throwing away money. Managers then wonder why no benefit comes from the money they spend on training.

Grass-roots education creates a common language in an organization. One reason why the Six Sigma program is so successful at General Electric is that everybody understands the basic principles and speaks the same language.

In any organization, you must teach a common language. Recently I met with the vice president of quality of a European automaker. I asked him, "Do you have a quality slogan?"

He said, "What do you mean?"

I said, "What is your quality policy? What do you aim to do with quality?"

He said, "We want to produce the best results, the best quality products."

I said, "Okay, fine." I pointed to the other four people in the meeting and said, "These are the four people who report to you, right?"

He said, "Yes."

I said, "Do you mind if I ask each of you separately a critical question?"

He said, "Fine."

So I took those five people and spent five minutes with each of them and asked them: "What is your quality policy?" Each of them gave me a different answer. That shows a lack of a common business language. Here is the top manager of quality in the corporation and the four senior managers who report to him, and they give me five different answers to the same question. Each of them was telling me, "This is what the company wants to achieve." They had no quality goals.

Cross-Functional Capability

Talents need training and education that suit them where they are at the moment. They need a different kind of training customized to their needs. Suppose, for example, that I am a Talent in finance. What kind of cross-functional training do I need to work well with people in marketing? If I am a Talent in marketing, how can I work effectively with people in design? Suppose we need to come up with a new car design. Most of the time marketing develops the information, saying, "This is what the customer wants. Give it to the designer." The two never work as a team. My goal as a cross-functional Talent would be, "Hey, I am already in marketing, so in this meeting I don't have to prove what I know about marketing; rather, I will try to find out what the design engineer, manufacturing people, and the finance people are talking about." The aim is to create a cross-functional Talent team.

The best Talents have cross-functional capabilities. Within their system, they understand the roles of others and work well with different people. That is what I mean by "cross-functional capability." They can't do the jobs of other people — but they know how to work with other Talent in different functions. Again, talented people want to work in an environment where they face positive challenges. Talent enjoys learning other aspects of the business.

Support for Change

Getting a few people to support your ideas for change will motivate others to accept and rally behind those ideas. You have to find the right Talents who will understand the ideas for change that you propose. You have to present your ideas to those Talents to check the viability of the ideas. They may challenge the ideas and come up with better alternatives. After they commit, they will motivate others to accept those ideas.

Management must convince people that change will benefit them. In today's competitive world, organizations can't survive without constant changes of products, services, and strategies. If organizations don't survive, employees have to search for new jobs and have to struggle more. So management should convince its employees that change is beneficial to the organization as well as to its employees.

Unless everyone tries to make it happen, any initiative will lose its momentum. Many initiatives fail because management forces change on employees rather than educating them about what the organization plans to do. So, before you introduce change, find colleagues who will embark on the journey of change with you. Find people who support you and will help persuade others who may not be convinced that the change will benefit them. To achieve any goal, you need to be flexible and creative. Beyond talking about change in meetings, you need to show people how the change will benefit them.

Seven Laws of Fusion of Talents

Individual Talents often implode when they collide with other Talents. Organizations must create a bond among cross-functional Talents. The creative explosion of Talent occurs when there is a fusion of Talent. The power of fusion is in sharing ideas and challenging each other. In a challenging environment, conflicts of ideas may still happen, but typically Talents celebrate those conflicts because they result in creative and powerful solutions and cross-fertilization of ideas.

Seven laws facilitate this fusion of Talents.

1. Break the Ego Barrier
Breaking the ego barrier is a prerequisite for the fusion of Talents. Real Talents learn to suppress their egos. If you have an ego, you can't learn anything from others. A ten-year-old child may know something better than a forty-year-old professional. If you don't have an ego, you can learn from that child. Real Talents don't have an inferiority complex. They know that good information and knowledge can come from anybody at any level, and they are ready to accept those. To break the ego barrier, you have to be open-minded.

2. Burn Any Jealous Attitude

Losing your jealousy is another important requirement in fusion of Talents. When people have jealousy, they won't want to share information or knowledge with others. They have the fear that if they share knowledge, somebody will know their secret of success and may succeed them. Sometimes due to jealousy, people share wrong information, which is very harmful. Real Talents don't have a jealous attitude. They encourage others to perform their best by sharing good knowledge and good information.

3. Build Trust

Without trust, people can't work together effectively. Without trust, people can't share knowledge or information. Real Talents want to build trust because they know that in today's competitive world it is impossible to succeed without a talented team. And to build a talented team, you have to build trust.

4. Simply Respect Each Other

Talents don't have any barrier of age, color, race, sex, or income. Anybody may be a talented person. Similarly, within the organization, anybody at any level may have talent. But real Talents respect each other. They give value to other Talents. There may be differences of opinion, but they respect each other.

5. Focus on Organizational Success
Rather Than Individual Success

Real Talents focus on organizational success before individual success. For example, Michael Jordan always worried about how he would win a game rather than how many baskets he would make. He knew that if his team won, he would be honored. Real Talents have a sacrificing attitude for greater success.

6. Share Responsibility

Sharing responsibility is one of the important factors for success in a team game. When there is a team, everybody on that team should share the responsibility of success and failure. When a group deci-sion is made, everybody in that group is responsible for that deci-sion. Before the decision is made, everybody can argue or criticize; but after the decision is finalized, real Talents don't want to pass on responsibility to others.

7. Embrace Failures As Well As Successes

Success or failure is just an outcome. There may be failure, but that is part of the game. Real Talents accept failure, analyze that failure, and learn from that failure. They don't blame each other when fail-ure happens. You should accept failure and learn from it. Albert Yu, senior vice president of Intel's Microprocessor Products Group and the person responsible for stoking the innovative engines of the world's semiconductor superpower, says:

> There is a tremendous power in glorious failure. The infamous Pentium flaw in 1994 was devastating and we went through all the stages of grief—denial, anger, and acceptance. It was in-credibly painful to the company, and to me personally. But we managed to become better as a result. It marked a real tran-sition. I'm a different person today. I've beefed up the way we validate our technology before it gets out the door. We went from having a product-engineered orientation to a consumer orientation. We all recognized that the problem threatened the image of Intel. We had real teamwork and came through the crisis together. Now we know that we can respond to any crisis 10 times faster than before.

Why Are the Seven Laws of Fusion So Important?

Why should Talents observe the seven laws of fusion? Talents typ-ically observe these laws, although some extremely talented people ignore one or two of them. They may break two or three of these laws regularly. Talents sometimes have tremendous egos.

These seven laws are like traffic laws. You may have speeding laws, for example. Some drivers don't obey speed limits. They think they are above the law or that the law doesn't pertain to them. Same thing with Talents. Talents are not robots. Talents are people. So if you are a manager, and you have a very egotistical Talent, your first law says, "Break the ego barrier." But if your Talent is very egotistical, what can you do?

Talents have to work on their weaknesses. I suggest to these Talents, "Yes, you are very talented, but you need to work with five other talented people." This is why it is called the "fusion of Talent." Fusion occurs when Talents collectively work together as a team.

If you have a violator, do you blow the whistle? Should a manager act like a coach or referee? One Talent needs to serve as a team captain and remind the team members constantly of what matters most, why they are working, and what good things are happening. Often people forget. We start to blame each other and talk negatively. Rather than talk about people negatively, explain the negative in a positive way with a positive attitude. If I only complain about what you are doing wrong and do not recognize what you are doing right, after a point, you will say, "This is not working out. Every time I talk to you, you complain." But if I say, "I like what you did here and here, but I want you to work on this element and make it better," this is very encouraging. Rather than react negatively, you might say, "Let me think about it." So, you can't act like a policeman — you have to drive out fear.

Drive Out Fear   Why do people have so much fear at work? Why does fear occupy such a prominent position in many organizations? Why does the "culture of fear" dominate many workplaces?

The culture of fear suggests that it is dangerous to speak the truth, that people are to blame for losses, that goals are not achievable, that people can be abused and abased for failure, and that competency and contribution are not rewarded. The culture of fear gets in the way of everything worthwhile. Growth stops, change stalls, morale sinks. Good people leave, and new good people stay away. People see the business as a zero-sum game where value is extracted from people as they are compelled to give up their time, energy, youth, and even their health. To force cooperation, the company applies duress.

In a company with a healthy culture, the value that the company brings to market is not extracted but rather created. Employees are not compelled to cooperate; they cooperate joyously because the work is satisfying, the products are a source of pride, and the community grows. In talent work, the only raw materials are inspiration, inventiveness, and work. A culture of fear is all wrong for creative work; a culture of fear is ultimately self-defeating because people leave and the company dies or is acquired.

Beyond avoiding a culture of fear, you have to build a positive culture of safety so that people can take some chances and make changes. Resistance to change can be fierce. It can also be subversive and destructive. Against this, managerial coercion is no match. You can't make proactive change happen; the best you can do is help it to happen.

Inevitably, the change you urge upon your people requires them to abandon their mastery of the familiar and become novices again. People can make this change only if they feel safe. The safety that is required for essential change is a sure sense that employees will not be mocked, demeaned, or belittled as they struggle to achieve new mastery. Change is defeated by name calling, irony and sarcasm, pointed criticism, personal mockery, public humiliation, exasperation, managerial tantrums, and eye rolling. To make your organization receptive to change, you need to replace disrespect with a clear sense that all people are honored for the challenge they take on. During change, every failure has to be treasured for the lessons it imparts, and the person who fails must be treated as a hero. Failure gains that person more respect, not less. To succeed in times of important change, you have to make it okay to fail. No honest failure will ever cost anyone respect.

I learned the hard way how to approach the negative with a positive — and that has made all the difference in my life and career. When I first came to the United States from my homeland, at the beginning of my career I did things totally differently. I was talking to people straight out and experiencing tremendous pushback. Once I was volunteering my time in a professional society and coming up with some of the best ideas, but none of them was getting approved. A friend of mine — a middle manager in a large corporation — observed me and said, "Rather than do it that way, try this — rephrase your suggestions when you present." He gave me this most valuable advice, and I followed it. In two years I became the chairman of that society.

When Talents violate these seven laws, they experience pushback instead of pull. People work against them, not with them. People resist their ideas rather than support them. Consider the following statement. "You can't tell anybody anything. You can only lead them to self-discovery." If you accept the truth of this statement and behave accordingly, you will discover a marvelous new acceptance of your ideas, even from the stubborn ones.

I suggest that these seven laws be put on a poster and displayed on walls. People need to see the rules of the road if they are trying to drive by them. In Talent environments especially, people must know the rules of the road to avoid clashes and crashes. When Talents live and work by the laws of fusion, they willingly share responsibility and respect other people. Talent can be anybody. The major weakness of some Talents is they don't trust other people. They are very talented in something, but they may not trust another person with their idea because they fear that somebody might steal it.

They forget that real Talents don't steal ideas. Michael Dell did not become who he is today by stealing from others. He had innovative ideas of his own. Real Talent comes up with genuine ideas. When you are working with ten other Talents, you should trust that they will not take your ideas. Grant trust, and you will receive trust.

Launching an Idea Bank

Encourage employees to deposit their best ideas in an idea bank. Reward them based on the power of their ideas. Good ideas can come from any level. Many intelligent men and women have great ideas, but they don't share their ideas with management due to fear. If the idea bank exists, any employee can share her ideas. If a proper reward system is set for depositing good ideas, many good ideas will surface, resulting in constant revolutionary change.

An idea bank is a place where any employee can deposit ideas. The important factors of an idea bank are trust, safety, and confidentiality. When employees know that they will not be cheated by the bank, then they will deposit their best ideas. Some organizations don't get good ideas from their people due to fear. If there is an idea bank, no good idea is lost, and the best ideas are implemented.

Reward employees for depositing ideas in the idea bank: Offer instant monetary reward for good ideas. Also offer a percentage of cost saving or profit sharing that comes with the implementation of an idea. Give awards and recognition. Consider promotion to the next level. These incentives encourage employees to deposit ideas.

When employees know that they will be properly rewarded for good ideas that are implemented, they will be more eager to bring more new ideas. Many companies have a fantastic idea bank concept. In theory, when your idea is implemented, you get some percentage of what the company makes out of it. But in reality companies tend to be very strict about paying or otherwise rewarding the people who come up with such ideas.

In contrast, at IDEO, the idea bank works well because it is independent of the company. In *The Art of Innovation,* author Tom Kelly writes about this innovative company. At IDEO, judges decide the worth of an idea. They may say, "It is a phenomenal idea, but it just doesn't apply here" or "We implemented that idea. This employee already copyrighted it, so let us pay him as we promised." If all employees embrace the idea program and make it an independent unit — meaning that unit does not report directly to management — they will make their own judgments, review all ideas, look at them, and see what they can do about them. They will interview all of the people who submit ideas, and if a person's idea is implemented, that person gets a reward.

Talent will rarely leave a company with a good idea bank. But, often politics is involved, and ultimately all of the workers are giving good ideas but are not being rewarded for them. So after the first or second time, they don't want to give any more ideas.

You need to create an independent body so that employees can deposit ideas and know that if their ideas are in demand they will be properly compensated. A lot of big corporations have a suggestion box that is totally useless. When employees submit an idea, managers may say, "No, it wasn't your idea." Or, they simply change the idea slightly and say, "This is not exactly like your idea." They take the employee's idea, change it a little bit, and then implement it. To me, that is violating what was promised. One of my friends fought for nine years to be compensated for a suggestion. Luckily, two of his senior managers supported him, saying "Absolutely this was a unique idea." Finally, after nine years, he was compensated.

The idea must be more concrete than somebody simply saying, "Could you make a car like the PT Cruiser?" I am talking about coming up with the whole plan in detail. "This is the way the car should be." As soon as you know that the idea is excellent, pick the person's brain to determine what potential the idea has. If the idea is feasible, then implement it and reward the person whatever you promised.

Honeywell Chairman and CEO Larry Bossidy said, "They had good ideas and knew how to present them, but they had not been prepared to execute. So we tried to give them generous severance packages and help them land on their feet. Nevertheless, the experience was painful for everyone involved." Employees often come up with an idea, but they don't know how to implement it. In a fusion of Talent, a team of Talents takes the idea from concept to delivery.

7 Talent Development Budget

In this chapter, I explain the importance of establishing a Talent development budget (TDB) that accounts for the costs of attracting, holding, replacing, training, and developing Talent. I propose a value-driven cost structure that measures the quality of work performed against the quantity of work performed. I recommend having a contingency plan for key Talents.

Special budgets for special people may send shock waves through an organization. Most organizations have been struggling to reduce inequities due to past discriminatory practices. Now if you propose a budget to deliberately increase inequities between classes of people, this new notion will encounter resistance. The sooner you face such resistance head-on by creating a highly visible TDB, the sooner you can get past this barrier.

Every organization should have a TDB. Without one, senior managers might complain: "I can't afford to send this person to this conference" or "I can't hire these people because I don't have any money." They face that challenge because they have a production budget and a cash budget, but not a TDB.

For growth, the talent development budget is more important than any other budget. All organizations, regardless of size, should prepare a TDB for the long term as well as for the short term. The long-term TDB may be prepared for more than one year to allow sufficient time to plan major expenditures for acquiring Talents, keeping Talents, and training Talents. This budget may help to determine the goals of the organization.

By preparing a TDB, organizations improve effectiveness and avoid poor allocation of resources. After an organization sets its goals, it can estimate how much to spend on acquiring, holding, and developing the Talents to meet the goals. A shortage of key Talent will lead to severe problems. If management spends more money in one low-priority area of business, the whole business suffers. Often Internet startup companies spend lots of money in advertising, which puts a company into a deep financial hole. Similarly, organizations cannot bear excessive costs on Talents.

A TDB is not the same as a training and development budget. A training and development budget is not allocated for attracting and holding Talent or replacing Talent. For example, if your CEO quits and goes to a competitor, and you have no budget to replace that CEO, you suddenly must incur a significant, unbudgeted expense. If you don't have the budget, you don't know what to do when you suddenly lose a key person. And yet it is foolish not to anticipate losing key Talent occasionally. For example, when a Fortune 10 company announced its new CEO after one of its most successful CEOs retired, three other people in consideration quit immediately. They assumed that in the next ten to twenty years they might not have a chance to become the CEO of the same organization. So, they accepted positions in three different organizations. The company might have anticipated this, but if it did not have replacement costs budgeted at that time, it would have had to use unbudgeted funds, which is always awkward at that level. Even if it promoted internal executives to fill those positions, it would still incur a heavy replacement cost. Flawless hiring of key executives is one of the critical factors for success. To achieve flawless hiring, you must dedicate sufficient time to select the right people, hire them, and bring them into the organization. You have to invest a lot of money. You can't just put an advertisement in *Fortune* or the *Wall Street Journal* and be done. The CEO needs to be involved in interviewing candidates and talking with their references. If you are considering hiring me, for example, and I listed someone as a reference, I would expect you to call my reference and say, "I have interviewed Mr. Chowdhury. He listed you as a reference. Could you please spend a few minutes with me about him, or could I meet you in person to talk about him?" Most senior managers don't do that because it costs money.

Senior managers should have access to money in the TDB to recruit Talents or replace Talents who leave. The cost of attracting and holding Talent and the cost of replacing Talent are two critical costs beyond training and development. Typically companies place training and development costs within human resources; but they should spend more money to attract, hold, and develop Talent.

High-potential Talent should receive the lion's share of the Talent development budget. Suppose seven of us work at a manager level in seven different divisions. Of the seven, maybe two of us are identified by the company as very talented people. So, rather than allow each of us $5,000 each for training and development, the organization should spend more money on the more talented of the seven. Give them growth opportunities. Make a special case for top performers who are the future of the company. Of those seven people, if the five other people leave, the organization may not suffer as much as if the two more talented were to leave. The Talent development budget can be sufficiently flexible to allow different spending levels for different people. The resulting disparities may cause the human resources manager some difficulty because of the apparent inequities. But that is the nature of attracting and keeping Talent. Talents are free agents.

After a company sets its goals and knows its capability, its management can prepare a TDB and plan to fund its key resources to meet the goals. For example, if a company plans to implement a Six Sigma initiative, its management may set goals to train three thousand employees in two years, spend $2 million on training and developing key Talent, and save $20 million on the projects. After the company sets such performance goals, management then allocates budget money to be spent in that way.

Corporations now prepare production budgets, sales budgets, cash budgets, and capital budgets. It is very easy for managers to prepare those budgets because they can easily determine the value of hard assets such as machinery, buildings, land, and other physical resources. But they cannot so easily prepare a TDB because the value of Talent is hard to quantify.

Talent can make a significant difference in any business. For example, if you give the same brush and paints to an ordinary person and to a very talented painter, you will see the difference in their artwork. Similarly in business, outstanding Talent can produce outstanding results using the same resources. To meet their goals, managers should decide if they should bring in new Talents or train existing Talents. They should calculate the return on investment in attracting, holding, and training Talent.

A TDB has three parts:

1.   The cost of attracting, hiring, and holding Talent

2.   The cost of replacing Talent

3.   The cost of developing and training Talent

The costs of attracting and hiring include salary, benefits, and recruitment costs. Holding costs include salary, compensation, and all other benefits related to retaining Talent. Replacement costs include severance pay and all other benefits paid to Talents who will be replaced and all other costs associated with bringing in new Talents to those positions. Development and training costs include all costs related to training Talent.

The first part of the Talent development budget is the cost of attracting and holding Talent. A Talent may say, "I am doing this much work" and challenge you or threaten you, saying, "If you don't give me this, I will quit today. I have a much better offer." If you need that person in your organization, that is a sudden and unnecessary cost. If you don't have a budget, how can you spend the money? Often managers lose some of their best people over a small amount of money.

Spend money to keep a key Talent. If the Talent is demanding — if somebody with a high performance rating threatens to leave — management should spend money to keep that Talent. This "retention bonus" is like a re-signing bonus. If a Talent has been working with distinction for an organization for five years and has not been well rewarded for her achievements, she will look for a better offer. When she receives one, she may use that offer to negotiate a better deal with her current company. A retention bonus is not a bribe but more of an incentive to stay.

Employees who ask for more money must present a solid business argument. If you feel the argument is valid, then use the budget and spend the money, especially if you cannot afford to lose that Talent right now.

Calculating the true value of a Talent is not easy. Management should decide the value of a Talent based upon performance, success, and goodwill. Hiring and holding good people with the right value are challenging. It is difficult to determine, for example, the exact value of your company's president. Difficult though it may be, the art of determining the value of Talent and preparing a TDB will be the key to success.

Value-Driven Cost Structure

You can determine the acquisition and replacement cost of Talent using a value-driven cost structure. The cost of Talent is a variable cost because Talent cost always changes. For example, the quality of work performed is more important than the quantity of work performed.

When Talents are seen as a fixed cost, they will leave. Talents should be seen as a variable cost. Most year-end bonuses depend on how many problems you solve temporarily, but talented people who create long-term value should be rewarded more than those who create short-term value. Most organizations give a big bonus to the firefighters. Suppose I am a firefighter, and you are a fire preventer. You are trying to design the product in such a way that the defect would not exist in the first place. Both of us report to the same boss, and he comes to me saying "This is a problem. Can you please solve it within six months?" I solve the problem. You say, "I can't solve this problem in six months. I need nine months to a year." But when you solve the problem, that defect will never come back because you will solve it by eliminating the defects from the root. In most cases, our boss will reward me instead of you. Your reward should be five times more than my reward. As it is, there is no reward for you, even though you are the true Talent.

The cost of Talent is highly variable. Organizations should pay their people based on a performance measurement unit, the evaluation of performance being the key element for determining salary. Performance should be based upon the quality and quantity of work. Often, managers analyze short-term operating performance but don't assess long-term value, and so they don't know how much to spend to bring in talented people. *Value* here means the price you pay for Talent relative to returns on your Talent investment.

Because there is no definitive market value for Talent, it is hard to hold good people with the right value (price tag).

Performance measurement varies for different activities. For example, you cannot use the same measurement or "metrics" in design engineering as you use in sales and marketing. In the design and engineering department, performance is measured against optimization of design, defects rate, customer's preference, and satisfaction. In the sales and marketing department, performance is measured against percent of sales volume increase against cost of sales.

Determining the acquisition and replacement cost of Talent and the total value of Talent is an art, not a science. It's never easy to determine the value of the people in an organization. When an organization wants to acquire new Talents, management should estimate how much it should spend to acquire those Talents by calculating the value of those Talents from past success and any goodwill created by the Talents. Organizations should measure the performance of their Talents. Based upon the performance and past success and goodwill, management should put a price tag on Talents. If managers want to acquire new Talents who don't have any experience or past success, they should implement a flexible, performance-based salary structure.

Contingency Plan for Talents

Hiring talented people is costly; in fact, the hiring process itself is costly and time consuming. There is a time gap between losing and hiring Talent. Opportunity loss is large for an organization. As the gap becomes bigger, loss becomes bigger. An organization's goal should be to minimize this gap.

Managers can minimize losses that occur during this time gap by having a standby team, making a proper contingency plan, and accelerating the hiring process. If you don't have a contingency plan, you will lose much time and money. The time gap between when you lose a person and when you hire a person will widen. It might widen to even three or four months. This gap represents a high opportunity cost, a huge opportunity loss. A contingency plan can reduce the damage from a loss of a key Talent. Once a friend called to tell me his number one man in Japan had just quit. My friend had a meeting with a client, and the employee who just quit had managed that client's account. "We are trying to expand our consulting service within this client, and, now, our lead guy is gone. Can you assist me in any way?" Luckily, I found somebody from our office to support my friend. If he had had a contingency plan, he would not have been so desperate. He would have just sent another person he was developing in the event that such a situation arose.

Management has to be ready for Talent shifts by having an alternative plan for key Talent. If you lose key Talent, you need to know what immediate actions you can take. If you have an alternative plan, you can minimize the impact of losing key Talent dramatically in terms of both time and cost.

In preparing a contingency plan, management should first identify its key Talents in each area. Then management should identify the next-level coworkers of those Talents. Encourage key Talents to share their knowledge and strategies with coworkers by facilitating learning. Involve next-level Talents in some critical projects to develop their strengths. Each organization should have a contingency plan so that if it loses people in key positions, others can step in immediately until the organization finds new Talent for those positions or those positions can be run without bringing in new Talents.

Well-conceived contingency plans will take care of most unanticipated staffing problems. How much money would a contingency plan save a large company like General Electric or Ford? It could save them millions of dollars. After one manager quit one of the leading U.S. automaker's profitable division, it suffered badly.

The Power of Developing Talent

When John Martin, CEO of Taco Bell, applied the power of developing people, his company grew exponentially. He notes:

> Every business is faced with a mandate of reducing costs while improving service. To become more service oriented and competitive, you need a workplace full of people who are empowered, self-sufficient, and highly motivated. Where can you find a work force like this? The answer is that you don't find it—you build it by providing your people with the tools, training, environment, and freedom they need to take charge. You build it by trusting that people have a strong desire to succeed. Why don't more companies do this? Fear. I know firsthand what this fear feels like. At Taco Bell, we spent years doing everything possible to keep our workers "under control," which resulted in high turnover, low morale, and slow growth. Fortunately, we recognized that our company would only go as far as our people would take us.

Martin recalls that in the 1980s, Taco Bell was in trouble. The company had experienced several years of negative sales growth. The stores were dark, menus limited, and advertising flat. The industry joke was that Taco Bell was such a well-kept secret that most people thought it was a Mexican phone company. "When my management team came on board, we began a change, starting with the way we listened to and responded to our employees and customers. We asked them what they wanted, we listened, and we realized that the products, systems, and prices that may have served us well in the past wouldn't satisfy our customers in the future. Following extensive market research, we implemented the first phase of our value program and turned our business upside-down to give our customers better quality, better service and greater convenience — and all at a lower price."

With the help of new technology, Taco Bell moved much of the slicing, dicing, and cooking that took place in the back of its restaurants to consolidated sites to allow employees to focus instead on final product assembly and service. Martin reports:

> These initiatives helped ensure food quality, order accuracy, speed of service, enhanced safety, and improved quality of life for our people. The key to our success is the empowerment we have given to our people. Our empowerment philosophy is based on the premise that to change what people believe they can do, you must first change their experience. We felt that our people could do far more than our industry gave them credit for. If we were serious about reaching our goals, we could either build a work force of unmanageable proportions, or we could create an environment that encouraged self-sufficiency and empowerment. We chose the latter. We committed ourselves to leveraging the talent of our people, and the more responsibility we gave them, the more they wanted. At every level, our people exceeded our expectations. They were turned on by the opportunities we presented and inspired by the challenges.
>
> We are striving to break down the functional silos that limit what our people have been told they can do. Today we are seeing more initiatives coming from the field. By empowering our people, we have sent the message that everything within our business is fair game.

We are creating a rich pool of highly-confident, self-sufficient, empowered individuals. I urge you to instill an entrepreneurial spirit within your organization. And when you do, you'll discover a tremendous new world of performance, prosperity, and personal reward.

Summary

The notion of having a substantial special budget for a special class of people, Talent, will be a new, uncomfortable notion for many organizations. Most organizations have been struggling to achieve equity, not disparity. The preparation of the TDB will be a clear signal that some people are going to be treated differently. It will be an important step in breaking down barriers to the changes necessary to compete in the Talent Era.

8 Return on Talent

Why are effective managers always interested in their return on investments? Why do they want to know who in the company is driving return on investments? Why should they care about measuring return on investments in Talent? What is the correlation between Talent and return on investments?

In this chapter, I introduce the concept of return on Talent (ROT). For decades, organizations have used key metrics like ROI (return on investments) and ROA (return on assets) to determine value. But, in the future, more organizations will use the measurement of ROT. Current business measurement equations merely measure the use of financial capital, but ROT measures the return on human capital. To calculate ROT, you simply divide a valuation for the *knowledge generated and applied* by your *investment in Talent.*

$$\text{ROT} = \frac{\text{Knowledge Generated and Applied}}{\text{Investment in Talent}}$$

Before we talk about calculating ROT, let us talk about the two key components of ROT: (1) knowledge generated and applied and (2) investment in Talent.

Knowledge Generated and Applied

Knowledge may be described as the "hidden" assets of an organization. Knowledge measurement relates to several factors that directly relate to business success — factors such as sales growth, profit growth, EPS growth, innovation growth, customer satisfaction, service quality, customer loyalty, customer retention, employee retention, new product development, product defect reduction, product failure rates, resources utilization rate, learning rate, number of patents and trademarks, and copyrights or new brands. By monitoring these factors, organizations can measure their knowledge assets and evaluate performance. By measuring knowledge accurately, management can better manage Talents. Proper valuation of knowledge helps an organization to know the ROT, which reflects the profitability of the investment in Talent.

Putting a price tag on knowledge generated helps a manager to quantify results. Talents generate knowledge, which is one of the greatest assets in the global economy. True knowledge brings creativity and innovation and adds value to the company. Knowledge has become a key production factor, like raw material, buildings, and machinery. Companies that measure the knowledge generated and applied by their Talents can make their investments in Talent more profitable. Companies cannot improve what they don't measure.

If you have talented people, knowledge generated is just one component. The most important contribution that Talents can make is in the area of knowledge applied. If knowledge is not applied, then the company loses most of the market value of that knowledge. So, whatever knowledge a talented person generates and applies during the year divided by how much I invest in that person gives me the ROT value. If certain talented people generate many innovative ideas but never implement any of them, they fail to generate any ROT value because the return for the company is nothing.

Knowledge generated increases with its effective deployment. Knowledge becomes an asset when it is captured and utilized effectively. Unless knowledge is effectively utilized or applied, it cannot generate any yield or ROI. For example, theories of physics have no value unless they can be applied for the benefit of society. Similarly, within the organization, generating knowledge doesn't add much value unless it is used in effective strategy formulation. Knowledge assets, like money or equipment, are worth cultivating only in the context of strategy. You can't define and manage intellectual assets unless you know what you are trying to do with them.

Investment in Talent

Without investment in Talent, an organization becomes stagnant. Organizations invest in technology, machines, and people. But in the twenty-first century, the most valuable investment is the investment in talented people. Management must invest in the right people, whose capability must match the needs.

Finding the right people is not only more difficult today but also more costly. Every company needs Talents in critical positions to operate successfully. If an organization can make the right investments in the right people, the organization will grow vigorously. Organizations cannot keep their top Talents without spending top dollars on them. Top Talents want top rewards: It is not just monetary, it also can be peer recognition.

Managers of Talent need to reward the right things. After you define the power of the knowledge generated, you can reward the Talent appropriately. Some managers become jealous of the Talent working for them, and so they shower rewards on the people who solve immediate problems (firefighters). If you manage the knowledge generation in a company, you have to make sure that the person who comes up with the brilliant ideas gets rewarded. You put a value on an idea and a higher value on ideas that are ultimately applied — and become a new reality. For example, right now we are using the Pentium IV or Pentium V processor. Eventually the Pentium VII processor will come out. Who is coming up with that technology? Talents at Intel who generate the next generation of chips should be recognized and rewarded. I am not talking about rewarding them the next day. Some applications of knowledge may take at least one or two years. But as soon as the knowledge is applied and the corporation gains market share, management must reward the Talent who made the innovation possible. Too often top executives and firefighters get all the social recognition and financial rewards.

Managers need a reliable tool for measuring return on Talent so they reward the right people. Imagine that over a three-year period, a Talent saves you $1 million, and your investment in her is minimal. About twenty people work with her, and these twenty people represent your Talent group or innovation function. Later, when they are doing something that saves you $100 million, they need to be recognized and rewarded more. But they likely won't be unless their manager measures the ROT value of this Talent pool.

Decreasing investment in Talent is usually a mistake. Such cutbacks bring about losses. To decrease the investment in Talent, senior managers must evaluate their expenditures on Talent regularly and consistently and learn about different areas in order to make wise strategic decisions on their investment in Talent.

To avoid creating an accounting nightmare, don't calculate ROT on every person, only on top Talent, maybe only about one thousand to two thousand people out of twenty thousand, consistent with XYZ analysis that X people make up 5 to 10 percent of the population but contribute 60 to 70 percent of the value. These people are the top Talents. Often middle managers are not necessarily talented, but several talented people report to them. Now, if you are trying to measure return on Talent, these middle managers won't care. It is essential that you explain to the managers, "We will invest more in our talented people."

Managers should use the ROT value to determine compensation. Compensation should be based on some balance between individual and team performance and contribution. So, your investment in one individual Talent might be as high as $250,000 a year. Suppose the investment in a CEO is about $5 million a year, but the board should keep her because of her intellectual contribution. As long as the CEO's return on investment is high (as measured in her company's profitability), she will continue to make $5 million a year, and no one will care because everyone wins.

Investment in Talent is critical, but Talent has to show results. You cannot invest more just because Talents ask for more. What energy level are they showing? What results are they getting? If you know that certain people represent the future of the company, invest more in them. Some Talents may complain, but you have to look at their performance objectively. If they come up with a compelling business case that shows the company will gain more for more investment, invest more in them. If you don't invest more, the Talent team might shut down the whole organization. ROT scores help you to invest the right amount in the right Talent at the right time.

You might double your investment in a talented team if you believe in its game plan. That's one of the keys to managing Talent. Most managers want to keep their investment small. In a downturn economy, they want to take away investment. They want to be very cautious. They don't want to invest more in Talent. But, they often overdo their cost cutting.

ROT Measurement

You can generate higher ROT values by increasing the numerator (knowledge generated and applied) or by decreasing the denominator (investment in Talent). Return on Talent is a function of knowledge and communication. A Talent generates more knowledge when all ideas and information can flow easily and multidirectionally.

ROT measures the payback from investment in people. ROT shows whether managers are hiring the right people and how effectively they use them to achieve business success. ROT can be a quantitative or qualitative measurement, based on management's viewpoint. Are managers getting the maximum payback every hour of the day on their investment? If managers want to see quantitative results, they must put a price tag on knowledge generated and results achieved.

Effective managers use ROT measurements to make their investments in Talent more profitable. ROT measurements help them to monitor performance, forecast opportunity, and determine the profitability of their investment in Talent. To make their investment more profitable, managers must constantly measure ROT, continuously improve ROT, and reshuffle Talents.

Companies that constantly improve ROT grow at a fast rate. Management can monitor the performances of individuals as well as teams. If knowledge assets are increased, then all other related factors like production and sales will increase as well. So corporations should try to improve ROT continuously to sustain growth.

High ROT leads to creative workforces, innovations, smooth processes, continuous product improvements, and improved communications. It helps management to be flexible, to capitalize on opportunities, and to keep pace with the changing climate. Talented people influence those around them, and their knowledge is shared over time. If managers expect them to achieve their maximum performance, and maximum return, they must not place them in routine jobs.

Talents create ideas and knowledge that may lead to tangible outcomes that can readily be measured and translated into monetary values. They also create ideas and knowledge that are intangible but are judged to have enormous value. What is intangible knowledge, and how is it measured? We call the things we can't measure in monetary terms "intangible." In the spirit of the definition of ROT, knowledge not yet applied is intangible. Only applied knowledge is tangible and measurable, as the phrase implies by its wording: *knowledge generated and applied.* The first challenge is to calculate ROTs for tangible, applied knowledge. The second challenge, which is obviously much more difficult, is to calculate ROTs for intangible knowledge generated. However, some form of measurement of intangible knowledge must be devised to enable a corporation to understand and properly determine the value of Talent.

The basic calculations of return on Talent focus on one Talent or one team at a time. In order to properly attribute financial changes to the right people, it is important to define all activities in terms of projects with a defined scope and a beginning, middle, and end.

Projects are a big deal. First, they are the means of getting things done. Lists of action items have never caused anybody to take action. Projects do. Projects require establishing goals and objectives, plans to achieve them, milestones. Monies and staff need to be allocated to projects. When these things are achieved, the corporation has a chance that some action will actually be taken. Without projects, there may be no ROT.

Second, projects provide a means of tracking a specific investment and the returns generated by that investment. Tracking is difficult in accounting systems that use general funds and allocations of monies in and out of the general funds. Activity-based costing (ABC) accounting simplifies the process of tracking costs and returns related to a given project.

Return on Talent (ROT) needs to be put in a form suitable for calculating meaningful measures. Net dollars realized from knowledge generated and applied are defined as the gross dollars realized minus the cost of generating and applying the dollars. Gross dollars realized may reference revenues, cost savings, or cost avoidance.

Net (knowledge generated and applied) is defined as project value minus project expenses.

For ROT calculations, project expenses should include all costs directly related to a project except the fully burdened salaries of Talent(s), fully burdened salaries of other team members if any, and all other expenses.

Three Examples of Calculating ROT

Following are three examples of how to calculate ROT numerators.

Example 1: Tangible Knowledge Is Generated and Applied

Investment in Talent is the total of all costs directly related to the fully burdened salaries of Talent and other team members. During the first six months, a Talent spent money on the idea project using the idea seeding fund to buy laboratory equipment and materials.

She also spent her time on a product development program. She documented progress in a laboratory book every day. The documentation was sufficient for the patent attorneys to write the patent with minimal additional help.

Investment in Talent = $150,000 × Portion of Time Spent on Project

$$= \$150{,}000 \times \frac{6 \text{ Months}}{12 \text{ Months}} = \$75{,}000$$

Project expenses included:

Idea Seeding Fund = $10,000

Idea Cultivating Fund = $50,000

Patent Application = $25,000

Project Expenses = $85,000

Knowledge generated and applied has two distinct elements: (1) knowledge generated and (2) knowledge applied. Some estimate of the intangible value of the knowledge generated, the technology, and the patent might be assumed for accounting purposes, as might be the case if you were applying for a loan. However, its real value is not known until the knowledge is applied. In this example, the application was to sell patent rights to another company. The tangible value placed on knowledge generated and applied is the sales price.

The patent was issued in the United States in eighteen months and in the European Union nine months later. Shortly after the U.S. patent was issued, a Fortune 100 company approached the company expressing interest in the patent. After the normal bickering and negotiations, the company bought the U.S. rights for $1,000,000 and the EU rights for $500,000 contingent and payable upon EU issuing the patent.

$$\text{ROT} = \frac{\$1,500,000 - \$85,000}{\$75,000} = 18.86$$

Applied Knowledge Value = \$1,415,000

Example 2: Tangible and Intangible Knowledge Generated and Applied

A relatively new hire, Janet, who had not yet learned to keep her head down and not make waves, became frustrated about the amount of time she was spending working with the finance department to reconcile differences between time cards (not time clocks) and project charges. Both had several signatures verifying the correctness of the submissions. The human resources group was tracking them to prevent overtime violations that had caused problems before.

She decided to talk to some of the managers and supervisors signing off on the submissions. She immediately discovered that no one wanted to talk to her. She continued to push until she found two people who would talk to her. They both explained that they did not pay much attention to those things. Others had already reviewed and signed off on their correctness. Furthermore, they were terribly time consuming. There was one project time sheet and time card for each of the five hundred employees in the department. And they were submitted every week. Human resources was involved in an effort to avoid a repeat of overtime violations that had caused problems last year.

The two people whom Janet had gotten to talk with her were managers. One told her that he would change inputs from his subordinates to balance the times reported on the project time sheets with project plans. The other manager had just transferred from the quality office. She told Janet a related story concerning time card errors. He suggested that time cards should have only one, or at most two, signatures — one by the person doing the work and the other, if management insisted, by his or her direct supervisor. His analogy was the old notion that "if more than one is in charge, no one is in charge." He reasoned that if more than one person signed the card, everyone would assume that all was well and sign the card without ever checking it. In other words, if more than one person was responsible, then no one would assume responsibility.

Janet was appalled at the waste and excited about the opportunity. But her boss was not at all enthusiastic about her unassigned and unapproved initiatives. He advised Janet that she was in over her head and would damage her career if she persisted. She and her finance partner reduced the visibility of their pursuits but persisted.

They observed that they were doing the same kind of reconciliation that the other signatories were doing. They decided to determine how long it took them to do their reconciliation and to assume that all others in the chain were spending similar amounts of time creating errors in changing times to agree with planned time allocations. They determined that they were each spending four hours a week doing what they believed was non-value-added work. Worse, it wasn't even honest. Managers were moving times charged to projects that had time available, not necessarily to the ones that people had actually worked on. The employee didn't need to submit anything because it was ignored anyway. They assumed, for lack of data, that each of the six people who signed the time cards and the project reporting sheets spent about four hours per week for a total of twenty-four hours per week. And that was for just one of twenty departments. If all departments were requiring similar times, the total would be 480 hours per week — the equivalent of twelve professionals who could be doing value-added work.

This was too big to let go. Janet and her finance partner prepared a white paper explaining their findings. They even proposed a three-part solution: (1) Eliminate time cards for professionals and make the managers responsible for preventing overtime violations; (2) use the project reporting sheet for both work time and allocation of time between projects; and (3) have only the individual doing the work and his or her boss sign the project reporting sheet. They collaborated in allocating the times recorded.

Janet's boss reluctantly agreed to take the proposal to his boss. The finance boss resisted. He did not think the proposal would do anything other than make people mad.

Janet and her boss teamed to champion the proposal up through the management ranks in human resources. Eventually, the proposal was accepted and implemented. The savings were projected to be 7.5 work years at $40,000 fully burdened salary for an annual savings of $300,000.

Janet and her finance partner each received a bonus of $30,000 to be paid out over three years. The money was the tangible portion of their idea, which for so long seemed as if it would die without a hearing and remain an intangible idea. An unexpected additional benefit soon emerged. More people at even higher levels of management were beginning to suggest ideas for improvement. Some of the ideas helped improve the performance of the organization.

How much did the ideas improve the performance, and how much improvement was due to other factors such as a strong economy? No one knew.

Janet's original idea caused many things to happen. She felt that she was at least partially responsible for the excitement. But no one else seemed to remember what she did that triggered so much activity. Her intangible contributions went unnoticed. Indeed, her original recognition was forgotten until the vice president of human resources offered an out-of-the-box idea: to treat recruits like customers to be coddled rather than potential employees to be interrogated.

Janet and her partner estimated that they spent three months total work time — forty-five days each. Their salaries averaged about $60,000 per year each. So, for this period, the investment in both Talents was [$60,000 × 2] / 12] × 3 = $30,000.

$$\text{Team ROT Value} = \frac{\text{Project Value} - \text{Project Expenses}}{\text{Investment in Talent}}$$
$$= \frac{\$300,000 - \$0}{\$30,000} = 10$$

Applied Knowledge Value = $300,000 for 2 people or $150,000 each

Now, in this scenario, ROT value is based on a team rather than on individuals. Sometimes ROT value does not have to be calculated for individual Talent if multiple Talents are involved.

Example 3: Intangible Knowledge Generated and Applied

Calculating intangible knowledge is a big challenge. But we face it in everyday life. Think about how easy it is for a mathematics teacher to score a student compared with a literature teacher scoring a student. A mathematics teacher scores a student's problem based on either right or wrong. But a literature teacher scores based on her feelings and the writing style of an essay; and that does not necessarily mean that the essay is right or wrong. This leads us to think about the value of intangible knowledge generated, which most managers often ignore.

Mr. HR Idea made a suggestion to Mr. Director, a boss who was getting bad reviews for poor performance and poor management style. He was a bottom line–oriented, command-and-control-style manager. He had been through the corporate management style training twice. Still, he just couldn't behave as people wanted him to behave. He couldn't shake his twenty-year military background. Everybody loved him in social settings. But in the work setting, where he had heavyweight authority, he was indeed authoritative.

Mr. HR Idea suggested that the boss think about "Talent as customer and boss as supplier" of goods and services that meet the needs and wants of all his employees. He went on to suggest that the boss take a customer service class to learn some of the specific techniques that service people use to keep customers happy.

That simple suggestion had immediate effects on Mr. Director. He could follow disciplined prescriptions about how to behave. He did that for twenty years in the service. He was tentative at first, but some rapid positive reinforcement from his subordinates and his peers gave him ever-increasing confidence. He soon discovered that listening for understanding made a big difference and was fun. He learned a lot about what went on in the organization. After a few years, his employees voted him the "year's best manager" — not most improved, but the best. He glowed for the remainder of his working life.

How much was this intangible knowledge passed on to Mr. Director worth? Who knows? Probably millions of dollars! But it is so intangible. Mr. HR Idea wasn't voted "best" anything. He did not expect and did not receive any recognition.

To transform intangible ideas into tangible knowledge generated and applied, we need a way to measure intangible knowledge assets. Here is a seven-step process: (1) Determine what the knowledge or idea generated is; (2) identify the source or originator of the idea; (3) track the path of the idea from the source through all potential applications; (4) identify at least one application; (5) identify one or more persons pursuing the application; (6) determine how to measure the financial benefits of the idea; and (7) determine the financial value.

Don't worry about the details of the formula. Some ideas take only hours to generate and communicate, such as Mr. HR Idea's idea about regarding employees as customers. The transformation in behaviors was, of course, an application, but it was still intangible. The benefits in organizational financial performance need to be measured or, if not financial, some metric such as employee satisfaction or reduced turnover. Examine the metrics the organization uses to evaluate year-over-year performance, such as internal or external revenues, internal or external customer satisfaction, productivity, patents generated, widgets invented, services provided, and any others.

Determine the return in whatever metrics you can find to use. Financials are preferable, but alternatives are better than no measurement.

Summary of Three Examples

Tangible knowledge generated and applied: Both the ROT ratio and the net value of the applied knowledge are important. High ROT ratios do not by themselves accurately reflect value to the company or the value of the Talent. A low ROT with a very large applied knowledge value is more significant than a high ROT with a small knowledge applied value. The magnitude of the applied knowledge value is $1,415,000, and the ROT ratio is 18.86 for example 1. Both are large, making it clear that the value to the company is large.

Tangible and intangible knowledge generated and applied: In contrast to example 1, the knowledge applied and the ROT are both a modest $150,000 and 10, respectively. Clearly, the first example provides significantly more value to the corporation. Applied knowledge value and ROT are important indicators for judging contribution.

Intangible knowledge generated and applied: The intangible value of the change in Mr. Director's behavior was judged by the CEO to be worth millions, whether you can actually calculate the benefits or not. We don't need to quantify it. Mr. HR Idea's initiative made a big difference. We need more of them. On second thought, it might be an interesting exercise to try to turn what appears to be a very intangible value into a quantified tangible value by deploying the seven-step process.

Optimize ROT

To optimize ROT, place Talent in positions where they can generate a lot of revenue and focus their activities by defining projects that can be tracked through multiple year-end closings. If talented people are not working in positions where they can generate knowledge and create wealth for the company, they are misplaced. People establish their own brand on their own expertise, and their knowledge, skill, or information should be leveraged exponentially.

Corporations rarely think about leveraging their technical Talent. They don't know which knowledge can be leveraged. Defining ROTs of Talent projects and summing all of the projects in the corporation will help managers gain the knowledge they need to make informed decisions about investments. It will also help them appreciate the value of Talents by developing an objective database that demonstrates that 60 to 70 percent of the value is indeed generated by 5 to 10 percent of the people — the X people in an XYZ analysis. Segmenting work by projects will also help determine which 5 to 10 percent of the people are generating and applying knowledge of high value.

9 The Seven Secrets of Talent

The seven secrets of Talent can be remembered by the acronym *SECRETS:*

1. Search for the dream.

2. Evaluate your strengths and weaknesses.

3. Cultivate discipline and determination.

4. Render ideas and actions inseparable.

5. Embrace positivity.

6. Take a never-give-up attitude.

7. Show a "next" mentality.

1. Search for the Dream

The dream is very important. It is the vision for a company. It is a vision for you. Henry Ford had a vision. Jack Welch had a vision.

You should have a vision. Every great founder or leader had a vision. We always talk about vision when we talk about leadership. People who are Talents are always searching for the dream. If it is not their dream initially, they make it their dream.

America's measure of strength is that we do not celebrate success for long time. For example, one of Stephen King's novels became a huge best-seller for three months — and then it was gone. And he is forced to look ahead to his next project, his next success. Few entrepreneurial heroes stay long in the spotlight. To emphasize the point, in most developing countries like India, Bangladesh, Nepal, and Sri Lanka, when you achieve one big success, you become a national hero, and so you tend to lose the "urge" to search for the next dream. People embrace the success for so long that they lose their competitive advantage. Winning requires celebrating the success of the moment and quickly jumping to the next challenge.

As part of my search for the dream, I write books in the field of management and quality to share my thoughts with readers. The publication of each of my books was exciting for a few months. Then I began searching for the next thing to attempt to replicate that success. I always tell people: Your goal in life is not to touch the ceiling. I know you can touch the ceiling at any time. Your goal should be to touch the sky.

Suppose you have a goal to touch the ceiling, and I have a goal to touch the sky. I will definitely reach the ceiling and possibly reach somewhere between the ceiling and the sky. If your goal is to touch only the ceiling, you will never exceed that ceiling. To me, everything is touchable. I don't believe in "untouchables." That is a major strength that humans have compared to other living beings. If we're motivated, we believe anything is achievable.

Once when I was ten years old, my parents took me to the theater while visiting another country. As I watched the performance,

I recognized one of the actors; he was a major star at that time in that country. I told my parents, "I want to meet him after the show. I want to tell him what I liked and disliked about his performance." My parents thought I was crazy. They said, "There is no way. He will not meet with you." Finally, my father gave in and said, "Go ahead and try." So I tried. I waited and waited for him, but I never did get to meet him that day. But I found his mailing address and wrote him a two-page letter saying, "To you, I might be a nobody, but I want to tell you something about your acting. You should respect those people who watch your performance and offer feedback. They are the only reason for your fame."

He responded by writing me a five-page letter, saying, "This is the first time I have ever received such a letter. You taught me something. And I want to teach you one thing: Never . . . think you are nobody. You are somebody. I do respect you and the others who criticize my plays." Within the next year, I became friends with him. My parents were shocked and amazed.

That small incident at the age of ten marked a critical crossroads in my life. It gave me a great deal of confidence. When reading novels in my country, I used to write the authors. I developed my public relations skills by doing that. I was constantly thinking of ideas and implementing them. For example, I started the first computer magazine in Bangladesh. I was not a computer science graduate, but I thought the country needed such a magazine. At the time I received a congratulatory call from the president of the country.

Searching for the dream is very important. I urge young professionals around the world to have that kind of vision. There are times when you might have to challenge your balanced thinking because talented people tend to exhibit a nontraditional approach toward life. It was certainly a big surprise for my parents when they saw that letter from the actor. You don't win if you don't even try.

2. Evaluate Your Strengths and Weaknesses

Soar on your strengths and contain your weaknesses. Over time, you can transform some of your weaknesses into strengths and continue to contain and improve remaining weaknesses. And don't forget to continue to improve and build on your strengths to soar even higher.

Most people have an exciting dream early in life, but they lose it later in life. Even more people have a realistic life dream, but few ever believe in themselves. You need to believe in yourself and evaluate your strengths and weaknesses. Self-respect means not only respecting yourself, but also respecting your work, your home, and your community. Many dreamers don't know how to respect their communities or homes. They don't know how to balance these elements in their life. You have to know your strengths and your weaknesses. How can you turn those weaknesses into strengths? Work more on your weaknesses. Don't embrace your strengths — embrace your weaknesses and try to work on them so you can go to the next level.

Some people work on weakness in an area of strength but don't work on weaknesses overall. When I immigrated to the United States, everything was very different — different culture, food, and language. I have tried my best to adapt by working on my weaknesses. At first, I read a lot of American history books, but I didn't deal with many Americans. I was never raised with Americans in the first place, so I was hesitant to mix with Americans.

When I finally did mix with several Americans, what happened? Did I see some people who were racist? Yes, but so what? I didn't care. Always remember: All five fingers on your hand are not the same; similarly, every human being is different. Some are good, and some are bad. It is the same in my birthplace, too. In

Southeast Asia, the racism is based more on religion. You are either Hindu or Muslim. Over here it is black or white or Hispanic or Asian and so on. The point I am making is that I didn't give up. You can't let the fact that the world is not perfect keep you from achieving your goals.

To become successful, I have had to admit my weaknesses every day and work on them. In America, first-generation immigrants usually hang around with their own people. I disagree with that practice. If you go to India, I would advise you to mix with the people there. If you go there and hang around with the Americans, you will never learn the culture. You will never learn the Indian strengths and weaknesses. That is why Mother Teresa became so successful in India — she didn't live her life like a traditional nun. She wore the Indian sari dress, celebrated local culture, embraced local people, and became successful. That is why I emphasize working on weaknesses. We always think about our strengths, and we always forget about our weaknesses. True Talents always evaluate their weaknesses and try to transform those weaknesses into strengths.

3. Cultivate Discipline and Determination

Discipline and determination turn dreams into realities. Discipline is very important in life. I find that many entrepreneurs have phenomenal ideas and much passion. But they fail because they don't have any discipline. They come up with ten ideas, but they don't go for one idea with the right discipline. They are trying to do many different things, but the real talent is to focus on one at a time and make sure that it works. I am in a situation where I could take on fifty different projects, but I don't succumb to the temptation. I focus on one or two at a time. Whatever I do, I do my best, and when that is done, I do the next project. That is where the discipline comes in. After you make the disciplined choice, you need the determination to see the job through to completion. Determination is a show of heart.

4. Render Ideas and Actions Inseparable

Put your ideas into action. You might have the best idea, but if you don't act on it, it becomes just another idea. You have to act on your best ideas. Talented people always put their good ideas into action. If you are Talent, you don't just have the idea. You have the idea and an action plan. Acting on the idea makes you Talent.

I have mentioned projects several times. Turning ideas into projects is a good way to link ideas and actions. Projects have a beginning, middle, and end. Developing projects helps to build the discipline to take action. Projects are a way to get things done.

5. Embrace Positivity

You can choose to be negative or positive. As a human being, I have negative things to deal with, but I don't see them that way. I don't want to see anything in a negative light. When somebody tells me "no," I always take it as a challenge to turn "no" into "yes." That is my skill. I do it by first thinking positive. I am confident in myself. I am persistent. I always go back to the people who are telling me "no" and try to make them see the positive side. So, what happens? Consistently, they turn around.

People often make decisions based on emotion, combined with perspective. A colleague of mine in the consulting field is a very positive guy. Positivity is contagious. I always think that if I had an opportunity to spend two hours with anybody, I would spend them with this friend of mine. It wouldn't matter what we talked about because of the excitement and enjoyment I get from talking to this friend. Whenever I visit him, I see so many positive things — and those things influence me.

If you exude enthusiasm all the time, as my friend does, you can drag most people out of their funk. There are some exceptions. Some people seem to just stay in their funk. Let it go. Perhaps they are depressed over something you don't know about.

I want all the people associated with me to know that I care about them, and that is the only thing I strive for. I strive to lead a life where most people will say, "I enjoyed this man's company." How can I make them feel good? It doesn't matter what level they are. They might be in my business, they might be in my family, they might be in my community.

Part of being positive is treating people equally — treating them with respect, regardless of age, sex, salary, position, and so on. You need to respect and cooperate with other people. It is okay to have professional jealousy, but you must be jealous of the person's work, not the person. Often I have met people who are very talented, but they don't achieve much because they are jealous that someone else is moving forward with "their idea." They are so jealous they can't move. They cannot concentrate. The only thing they worry about is how the other guy is doing.

When eminent management thinker Charles Handy lost his father, the death changed his life. He realized that his father was like a local celebrity, a hero. Many people came to his funeral. They didn't come because he was Charles Handy's father; they came because his father was such a nice man. Charles said, "I doubt that many people will come to my funeral." This changed his life. Try to become more positive with other people, more loving, more forgiving. Positive thinking is extremely important for any success.

6. Take a Never-Give-Up Attitude

If I believe I can do something and decide to do it, I won't give up. Even if I don't achieve it for fifty years, I won't give up. How do you sustain such determination? It is in your heart. It is your passion. If you don't make it your passion, you will never do it. Billionaires have enough money right now. They could quit and be fine. But money doesn't matter to them. They have some goal in life that they want to achieve. The richest men and women in the world are always after something else, not just financial benefits.

So, never give up. Don't take "no" for an answer. To never give up, you need confidence and determination — the never-give-up attitude. Persistence is important. If you believe in yourself, the day will come when people will believe in you.

When I took on a challenging book project, many people told me "no" during the development phase. I didn't give up because I knew I could make it happen. So it didn't matter who told me "no"; I told people they would regret it if they did not participate in the project. I was confident in myself, and I was very persistent, too. One or two people told me "no" over two years ago. Afterward they said, "Subir, I cannot believe that you did it. This is wonderful." Yes, because I never give up. I could have taken the rejection personally, but I never did.

7. Show a "Next" Mentality

The "next" mentality is the perspective that now that we have achieved this concept or goal, what is the next one? It is a hunger for the next achievement. Once I was invited to talk to a group of Asian immigrants. They ranged in age from twenty-one to thirty. They could relate to me because I was a young immigrant, too. They asked me to talk about success. I said, "Raise your hands if you think I am successful." Almost all of them raised their hands. I then said, "If you ask me whether I am successful, I will tell you, 'Not at all. Not yet. I have too many things yet to accomplish.'" *Success* is such a relative term. Successful people's constant urge is to break the record of previous glory.

Examples are many. Whatever Thomas Edison had done before was never enough for him. He didn't stop there. Every successful individual I have ever met is going after "the next one." At age ninety, eminent management thinker Peter F. Drucker is always looking for "the next one." Every great leader has a "next" mentality. It doesn't matter what your focus is. Don't celebrate your success for a long time. Strive for the next success and for "next" thinking. Talent always strives for the next thing.

Example of the Talent SECRETS: Michael Jordan

To see how these seven secrets have been applied in one Talent's life, let's look at Michael Jordan as he relates his story "In Pursuit of Excellence" as published in the premier issue of *Personal Excellence* magazine.

1. Search for the Dream

I always had the ultimate goal of being the best, but I approached everything step by step using short-term goals. When I met one goal, I set another reasonable, manageable goal that I could achieve if I worked hard enough. Each step or success led to the next one. Each time I visualized where I wanted to be, what kind of person and player I wanted to become. I approached it with the end in mind. I knew exactly where I wanted to go, and I focused on getting there. As I reached those goals, I gained a little confidence every time I came through. It was all mental for me. I never wrote anything down. I just concentrated on the next step. I could apply that approach to anything I might choose to do. It's no different from the person whose ultimate goal is to become a doctor. All those steps are like pieces of a puzzle. They all come together to form a picture. If it's complete, then you've reached your goal. If not, don't get down on yourself. If you do your best, then you will have some accomplishments along the way. Not everyone is going to get the entire picture. Not everyone is going to be the greatest. But you can still be considered one of the best at what you do.

2. Evaluate Your Strengths and Weaknesses

Fundamentals are crucial. Everything I achieved can be traced back to the way I approached and applied the fundamentals, the basic building blocks or principles that make everything work. I don't care what you're doing—you can't skip fundamentals if you want to be the best. But some guys don't want to deal with that. They're looking for instant gratification, so maybe they skip a few steps. They're so focused on composing a masterpiece that they never master the scales. You can get away with it through the early stages, but it's going to catch up with you eventually. The minute you get away from fundamentals—whether it's proper technique, work ethic, or mental preparation—the bottom can fall out of your game, your schoolwork, your job, whatever you're doing. When you understand the building blocks, you begin to see how the entire operation works. And that allows you to operate more intelligently, whether it's in school, business, or even family. It sounds easy, but it isn't. You have to monitor your fundamentals constantly because the only thing that changes will be your attention to them. The fundamentals will never change. There is a right way and a wrong way to do things. Get the fundamentals down and the level of everything you do will rise.

3. Cultivate Discipline and Determination

I can accept failure. Everyone fails at something. But I can't accept not trying. It doesn't matter if you win as long as you give everything in your heart and work at it 110 percent. If you put in the work, the results will come. I can't do things half-heartedly. Because I know if I do, then I can expect half-hearted results. That's why I approach practices the same way I approach games. You can't turn it on and off like a faucet. I can't dog it during practice and then, when I need that extra push late in the game, expect it to be there. But that's how a lot of people approach things. And that's why a lot of people fail. They sound like they're committed to being the best they can be. They say all the right things, make all the proper appearances. But when it comes right down to it, they're looking for reasons instead of answers. You see it all the time in business. There are a million excuses for not paying the price. "If I was only given a particular opportunity" or "if only the boss liked me better, I could accomplish this or that." Nothing but excuses. That's not to say there aren't obstacles or distractions. If you're trying to achieve, there will be roadblocks. I've had them; everybody has them. But obstacles don't have to

stop you. If you run into a wall, don't turn around and give up.
Figure out how to climb it, go through it, or work around it.

4. Render Ideas and Actions Inseparable

I've always tried to lead by example. I never tried to motivate
by talking because I don't think words ever mean as much as
action. A picture carries a thousand words. So I tried to paint
a picture of hard work and discipline. Why not? If the person
out front takes a day off or doesn't play hard, why should anyone else? A leader has to earn that title. You aren't the leader
just because you're the best player on the team, the smartest
person in the class, or the most popular. No one can give you
that title either. You have to gain the respect of those around
you by your actions. You have to be consistent in your approach whether it's basketball practice, a sales meeting, or
dealing with your family. Those around you have to know what
to expect. They have to be confident that you'll be there, that
your performance will be consistent from game to game, particularly when things get tight. Ultimately, players can say anything they want, but if they don't back it up with performance
and hard work, the talking doesn't mean a thing. A leader can't
make any excuses. There has to be quality in everything you
do—off the court, on the court, in the classroom, on the play-
ground, inside the meeting room, outside of work.

5. Embrace Positivity

I never look at the consequences of failing. Because when you
think about the consequences you always think of a negative
result. If I'm jumping into any situation, I'm thinking I'm going to be successful—not about what happens if I fail. Some
people get frozen by fear of failure by thinking about the possibility of a negative result. They might be afraid of looking
bad or being embarrassed. I realized that if I was going to

achieve anything in life, I had to be aggressive. I had to get out there and go for it. I don't believe you can achieve anything by being passive. I know fear is an obstacle for some people, but to me it's an illusion. Once I'm in the game, I'm not thinking about anything except what I'm trying to accomplish. Any fear is an illusion. You think something is standing in your way, but nothing is there—only an opportunity to do your best and gain some success. My advice has always been to think positive and find fuel in any failure. Sometimes failure gets you closer to where you want to be. The greatest inventions in the world had hundreds of failures before the answers were found.

6. Take a Never-Give-Up Attitude

You have to stick to your plan. A lot of people try to pull you down to their level because they can't achieve certain things. But very few people get anywhere by taking shortcuts. More people gain success the honest way, by setting their goals and committing themselves to achieving those goals. Along the way, you also have to stand up for what you believe and hold on to your convictions. All the people I admire do that. They all created their own vision. And they didn't let anyone or anything distract them or break them down. They set an example and they led. Every home, every business, every neighborhood, and every family needs someone to lead.

7. Show a "Next" Mentality

A leader is also a person who has had past successes in certain situations and isn't afraid of taking the chance to lead others down that road again—someone who has a certain vision, an ability to look ahead or to anticipate what's coming. Set realistic goals—and focus on them. I ask questions, I read, I listen. I'm not afraid to ask anybody anything if I don't know. Why should I be afraid? I'm trying to get somewhere. My attitude is "Help me, give me direction."

If you know you are doing the right things, just relax and perform. Forget about the outcome. You can't control anything anyway. It's out of your hands. So don't worry about it. When you make a presentation in business, you may do all the things necessary, but then it's out of your hands. Either the clients like the presentation, or they don't. It's up to the client or the buyer.

Our society tends to glamorize individual levels of success without taking the entire process into consideration. What if you have a CEO with a great idea, but he doesn't have the people to make it happen? If you don't have all the pieces in place, particularly at the front lines, that idea doesn't mean a thing. You can have the greatest salespeople in the world, but if the people making the product aren't any good, no one will buy it. Managers, like coaches, have to find ways to utilize individual talents in the best interests of the company. It's a selfless process. In our society sometimes it's hard to come to grips with filling a role instead of trying to be a superstar. We tend to ignore or fail to respect all the parts that make the whole thing possible. Talent wins games, but teamwork and intelligence win championships. You have to transfer those skills, that drive, to whatever environment you're in. And you have to be willing to sacrifice certain individual goals, if necessary, for the good of the team.

Bibliography

Ashhenas, Ron, Dave Ulrich, Todd Jich, and Steve Hear. *The Boundaryless Organization: Breaking the Chains of Organizational Structure*. San Francisco: Jossey-Bass Publishers, 1995.

Bennis, Warren, and Burt Nanus. *Leaders: Strategies for Thinking Charge*. New York: Harper Business, 1985.

Bennis, Warren. *On Becoming a Leader*. New York: Perseus Press, 1994.

Champy, James, and Nitin Nohria. *The Arc of Ambition: Defining the Leadership Journey*. New York: Perseus Books, 2001.

Chowdhury, Subir. *The Power of Six Sigma: An Inspiring Tale of How Six Sigma Is Transforming the Way we Work*. Chicago: Dearborn Trade, 2001.

Chowdhury, Subir, ed. *Management 21C: Someday We'll All Manage This Way*. London: Financial Times Prentice Hall, 2000.

Collins, James C., and Jerry I. Porras. *Built to Last: Successful Habits of Visionary Companies*. New York: Harper Business, 1994.

Davenport, Thomas O. *Human Capital: What It Is and Why People Invest It*. San Francisco: Jossey-Bass, 1999.

Dell, Michael. *Direct from Dell: Strategies that Revolutionized an Industry*. New York: Harper Business, 1999.

Drucker, Peter F. *The Essential Drucker*. New York: Harper Business, 2001.

——. *Management Challenges for the 21st Century*. New York: Harper Business, 1999.

——. *The Frontiers of Management*. New York: Penguin Group, 1999.

Farren, Caela. *Who Is Running Your Career: Creating Stable Work in Unstable Times*. Austin, Texas: Bard Press, 1997.

Fitz-enz, Jac. *The ROI of Human Capital: Measuring the Economic Value of Employee Performance*. New York: Amacom, 2000.

Gates, Bill. *Business @ Speed of Thought: Using Digital Nervous System*. New York: Warner Books, 1999.

Ghoshal, Sumantra, and Christopher A. Bartlett. *The Individualized Corporation: A Fundamentally New Approach to Management*. New York: Harper Business, 1997.

Godin, Seth. *Unleashing the Ideavirus*. New York: Do You Zoom, 2000.

Grove, Andrew S. *Only the Paranoid Survive: How to Exploit the Crisis Points that Challenge Every Company*. New York: Currency Doubleday, 1996.

Gubman, Edward L. *The Talent Solution: Aligning Strategy and People to Achieve Extraordinary Results*. New York: McGraw-Hill, 1998.

Hamel, Gary, *Leading the Revolution*. Boston: Harvard Business School Press, 2000.

Hamel, Gary, and C. K. Prahalad. *Competing for the Future*. Boston: Harvard Business School Press, 1994.

Handy, Charles. *The Hungry Spirit beyond Capitalism : A Quest for Purpose in the Modern World*. New York: Broadway Books, 1998.

Heenan, Davida, and Warren G. Bennis. *Co-Leaders: The Power of Great Partnerships*. New York: John Wiley & Sons, 1999.

Hesselbein, Frances, Marshall Goldsmith, and Richard Beckhard. *Leader of the Future*. San Francisco: Jossey-Bass, 1996.

——. *Organization of the Future*. San Francisco: Jossey-Bass, 1997.

Hill, Linda A. *Becoming a Manager: How New Managers Master the Challenges of Leadership*. New York: Penguin, 1993.

Kanter, Rosabeth Moss. *Evolve!: Succeeding in the Digital Culture of Tomorrow*. Boston: Harvard Business School Press, 2001.

Katz, Donald. *Just Do It: The Nike Spirit in the Corporate World*. Holbrook, Mass.: Adams Media Corporation, 1995.

Kaye, Beverly L., and Sharon Jordan-Evans. *Love 'Em or Lose 'Em : Getting Good People to Stay*. San Francisco: Berrett-Koehler, 1999.

Kelley, Tom, with Jonathan Littman. *The Art of Innovation*. New York: Currency/Doubleday, 2001.

Kotter, John P. *Leading Change*. Boston: Harvard Business School Press, 1996.

——. *On What Leaders Really Do*. Boston: Harvard Business School Press, 1999.

Kouzes, James M., and Barry Z. Posner. *The Leadership Challenge*. San Francisco: Jossey-Bass, 1995.

Levine, R. Stuart, and Michael A. Crom. *The Leader in You*. New York: Simon & Schuster, 1993.

Peters, Thomas, and Robert H. Waterman. *In Search of Excellence: Lessons from America's Best-Run Companies*. New York: Warner Books, 1990.

Redstone, Sumner. *A Passion to Win*. New York: Simon & Schuster, 2000.

Roddick, Anita. *Business as Unusual*. London: Thorsons, 2000.

Rubin, Harriet. *Soloing: Realizing your Life's Ambition*. New York: Harper Business, 1999.

Senge, Peter M. *The Fifth Discipline: The Art and Practice of the Learning Organization*. New York: Currency/Doubleday, 1990.

——. Art Kleiner, Charlotte Roberts, Richard Ross, George Roth, and Bryan Smith. *The Dance of Change: The Challenges to Sustaining Momentum in Learning Organization*. New York: Doubleday, 1999.

Stewart, Thomas A. *Intellectual Capital: The Wealth of Organizations*. New York: Doubleday/Currency, 1997.

Tulgan, Bruce. *Winning the Talent Wars: How to Manage and Compete in the High-Tech, High-Speed, Knowledge-Based Superfluid Economy*. New York: Norton, 2001.

Welch, Jack, with John A. Byrne. *Jack: Straight from the Gut*. New York: Warner Books, 2001.

Yunus, Muhammad. *Banker to the Poor: Micro-Lending and the Battle against World Poverty*. New York: Public Affairs, 1999.

Acknowledgments

Every day I meet people in business, in community, in games, and in family who are talented individuals. These people inspire me to think differently and encourage me to celebrate every moment of life. They are the reason I wrote this book, and for this I am grateful to each of these people.

The idea for this book grew from a suggestion by my former editor Pradeep Jethi, of *Financial Times* in London. When I submitted to Pradeep the manuscript for my previous book, *Management 21C,* he urged me to continue my research on the theory of Return on Talent. After that book's publication in 1999, I received several requests from thought leaders, corporate executives, and above all readers from all over the world who were eager to know how to measure return on investment in Talent. When Pradeep left his editor job to go into entrepreneurial venture, he introduced me to another young and dynamic editor, Richard Stagg. As a result of Richard's continuous encouragement, I began documenting my thoughts. Pradeep and Richard, thank you for your early visions and continuous support. Your friendships are treasures to me.

A great talent who helped me understand how to take the right thoughts from my brain to the keyboard is Ken Shelton, editor of

Executive Excellence. In every conversation I had with Ken I learned something new. I feel a deep sense of gratitude to Ken for his enormous support, his hard work, and his help in refining the manuscript with integrity and a sense of quality.

My colleague and friend Dr. Barry Bebb is a phenomenal researcher. Barry challenged me and helped me to develop the Talent Scorecard. Barry, thank you for your hard work on the manuscript and your continuous challenge.

This is my sixth book in the past five years. In my writing career, I have never met a publisher like Jeff Pepper, who was involved with me on this project from day one. Jeff read every word of this book, working on weekends until 1 AM to challenge my thinking. It is any author's dream to have a publisher and friend like him. Jeff, I am eternally grateful to you.

Special thanks to my editor at Financial Times Prentice Hall, Jim Boyd, for his constant help and understanding.

I would like to express my gratitude to the editors, authors, and publishers of several prestigious newspapers, magazines, and journals, including *Harvard Business Review, Sloan Management Review, The Wall Street Journal, Fortune, Forbes, Financial Times, Business Week, USA Today, Executive Excellence, Personal Excellence,* and *Fast Company*. People of these organizations are great help to my research.

I am also grateful to my parents, Sushil and Krishna Chowdhury, and to my in-laws, Ashim and Krishna Guha, for their constant demonstration of love.

This book would have never been a reality without the support of my lovely wife, Malini. Her continuous intellectual thoughts are reflected on nearly every page of this book.

Index

About the Author

Subir Chowdhury is executive vice president at the American Supplier Institute, an international consulting and training firm. Prior to ASI, he served as a quality management consultant at General Motors Corporation. Hailed by the *New York Times* as a "Leading Quality Expert," Chowdhury was also recognized by *Quality Progress* of the American Society for Quality as one of the "Voices of Quality in the 21st Century."

Author of six books, Chowdhury's most recent international best-selling books include *The Power of Six Sigma* and *Management 21C: Someday We'll All Manage This Way*. His books have been translated into more than ten languages. He is frequently cited in the national and international media.

Chowdhury has received numerous international awards for his leadership in quality management and major contributions to the automotive industry. Chowdhury was honored by the Automotive Hall of Fame, and the Society of Automotive Engineers awarded him its most prestigious recognition, the Henry Ford II Distinguished Award for Excellence in automotive engineering. He also received the honorable U.S. Congressional Recognition. In 1999–2000, he served as chairman of the American Society for Quality's Automotive Division.

Chowdhury lives with his wife, Malini, and their daughter, Anandi, in Novi, Michigan.

The *Financial Times* delivers a world of business news.

Use the Risk-Free Trial Voucher below!

To stay ahead in today's business world you need to be well-informed on a daily basis. And not just on the national level. You need a news source that closely monitors the entire world of business, and then delivers it in a concise, quick-read format.

With the *Financial Times* you get the major stories from every region of the world. Reports found nowhere else. You get business, management, politics, economics, technology and more.

Now you can try the *Financial Times* for 4 weeks, absolutely risk free. And better yet, if you wish to continue receiving the *Financial Times* you'll get great savings off the regular subscription rate. Just use the voucher below.

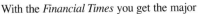

8 reasons why you should read the Financial Times for 4 weeks RISK-FREE!

To help you stay current with significant developments in the world economy ... and to assist you to make informed business decisions — the Financial Times brings you:

1 Fast, meaningful overviews of international affairs ... plus daily briefings on major world news.

2 Perceptive coverage of economic, business, financial and political developments with special focus on emerging markets.

3 More international business news than any other publication.

4 Sophisticated financial analysis and commentary on world market activity plus stock quotes from over 30 countries.

5 Reports on international companies and a section on global investing.

6 Specialized pages on management, marketing, advertising and technological innovations from all parts of the world.

7 Highly valued single-topic special reports (over 200 annually) on countries, industries, investment opportunities, technology and more.

8 The Saturday Weekend FT section — a globetrotter's guide to leisure-time activities around the world: the arts, fine dining, travel, sports and more.

For Special Offer See Over

FT FINANCIAL TIMES
World business newspaper